EXPLORING
NEW
FRONTIERS

EXPLORING
NEW
FRONTIERS

Navigating The Evolving Digital Landscape

Derek Osborn
Whatnext4u

LIBRI
PUBLISHING

First published in 2021 by Libri Publishing

Copyright © Derek Osborn

ISBN 978-1-911450-77-1

A CIP catalogue record for this book is available from The British Library

Design by Carnegie Book Production

Printed in the UK by Short Run Press

Libri Publishing
Brunel House
Volunteer Way
Faringdon
Oxfordshire
SN7 7YR

Tel: +44 (0)845 873 3837

www.libripublishing.co.uk

CONTENTS

ACKNOWLEDGEMENTS

This is the second volume of the 'Exploring New Frontiers' series and it builds on the previous volume and the earlier two series. All these books have been widely distributed, read and discussed throughout the postal, parcels and logistics world. This new volume has been collated in response to requests and encouragement from both readers and authors. My sincere thanks to John Sivak and all at Libri Publishing for their continued support and expert help.

All these contributions were written during the period of the global pandemic when authors were experiencing varying degrees of lockdown restrictions, hardships or stress and, at the very least, a significant change to most normal routines. I am very grateful to all these thought leaders, who have invested their time to share their insights and experience.

This volume is dedicated to the commitment and resilience shown by essential workers and everyone in the wider postal industry who continued to do their important work despite hardships and difficulties during the pandemic, and in particular to those who suffered severe illness or the tragic loss of a family member or loved one.

THE EDITOR

Derek Osborn is an enthusiastic, innovative and inspiring business coach, speaker, management trainer, forum organiser and workshop facilitator. Through his company, Whatnext4u, he works all over the world, especially in Europe, the Middle East, Africa, Asia and the Pacific – focusing on postal business strategy, investing in people (human resources), innovation and fresh thinking, developing future leaders, stakeholder engagement, and supporting those who are leading change – all with the main objective of ensuring *a more sustainable future for everyone*. He has wide experience and knowledge of the postal business, with 23 years in senior management in Royal Mail in the UK and now over 24 years working internationally across the postal industry. He is passionate about creating opportunities and platforms for collaboration to share knowledge and ideas and benchmark best practice so as to promote the industry externally, develop capability, encourage learning and foster innovation. Derek has coached many people and organisations, including governments, national postal operators and other postal stakeholders, working with them to formulate innovative strategies, improve operations and efficiency, develop greater customer orientation, strengthen people engagement, and to lead change and transformation. He specialises in devising and delivering bespoke senior executive programmes, roundtables, regional postal business forums and benchmarking workshops. He has designed and facilitated strategy-development workshops, using books like this and previous ones as texts to help focus thinking and trigger productive discussions. Previously, he co-edited three volumes of 'The Future is in the Post', and edited three volumes of 'Reinventing the Post' and the first volume of 'Exploring New Frontiers'. He can be contacted at derekosborn@whatnext4u.com.

INTRODUCTION

Derek Osborn

Editor

Entering the 2020s, the world is facing many global challenges. Some of them are unexpected and unplanned for, such as the coronavirus pandemic; others, like climate change and environmental sustainability, are not new or unexpected but are increasingly becoming recognised more clearly and the need for collective global action felt more acutely. In addition, demographic challenges, political instability, food and water insecurity, poverty, inequality and social deprivation, and faltering economies continue to inspire development initiatives with the aspiration to improve the quality of life for all people and build a better world.

Against this backdrop, huge technological advances have continued apace, fuelling the digital revolution so that many people are always online, along with rapid development of artificial intelligence, autonomous solutions and many other new technological explorations. This digital revolution was already impacting on all aspects of our daily lives in many ways and now the pace of this transformation has accelerated markedly as a result of the measures imposed to combat the pandemic, in particular the restrictions placed on physical movement and direct human contact during widespread and extensive 'lockdowns'.

One outcome of the pandemic has been to reinforce the value of the postal sector as an essential service provider. It has been widely valued and appreciated for being able to maintain delivery services for letters and many more parcels – at continuous peak levels – and essential medical, vaccine and pharmaceutical supplies, financial services, groceries and social care.

In previous thought-leadership books on the postal sector, we have charted the dramatic changes in recent years as postal operators have been driven to adapt to changing market needs and stay relevant for new generations – for their own survival. The series on 'The Future is in the Post' and 'Reinventing the Post' showcased many ways in which the sector was evolving to serve customers and stakeholders by doing things differently and diversifying – very often transforming their business or organisation.

The first book of this 'Exploring New Frontiers' series focussed on how the breakdown of sector boundaries, alongside digital disruption, was reshaping the postal industry. This meant that simple definitions or descriptions of sectors now had to be revisited and revised. The postal sector was morphing into something much broader, which might loosely be called the postal, parcel and logistics industry – although even that may not fully cover the breadth of a sector that also delivers government services and engages in a wide range of financial and payment services, and activity across the whole e-commerce value chain and eco system – as well as providing social services and disaster relief in some cases! The essence of the traditional post office as a trusted public service with a universal obligation to serve all citizens, businesses and communities permeates each new incarnation.

Now that the pandemic has propelled us further, deeper and faster into an all-pervasive digital world, we are all recalibrating our behaviour, lifestyle and consumer habits. So, it is in this context that contributors to this book have reflected on how the sector is navigating this evolving digital landscape. They are sharing their insights and experience from many different perspectives on the sector and from different parts of the world, which ensures a richness in the diversity of thinking. As with previous books, I have tried to edit their writing sufficiently (I hope) to ensure they are accessible and readable, whilst also enabling readers to hear their authentic voice articulated through their own words.

So how should you use this book? You are welcome to read it from cover to cover but you can also look at the contents page and dip into it here and there. Each contribution is self-contained and can be read on its own, although they are also broadly grouped into sections, recognising that there will be overlaps and gaps. At the end of each contribution, you will find two questions for thought and discussion. These questions are there to trigger discussion and further thoughts on the topic, and reflect the fact that no-one has all the answers, most of the topics are complicated and, if we are to move our industry and our organisation forward, we must take time and effort to wrestle with these important issues.

So whatever your interest in the sector or your position in your organisation or business, I would like to encourage you to use the book to find relevant questions to ask yourself and your colleagues, whether it be formally in board meetings or workshops, or informally during coffee breaks or with friends. We can learn so much from listening to the experience of others and having robust discussions – there is even a chance we can change our views and find some new and valuable idea for our role or our business.

As well as the questions at the end of each chapter, as you read this book you may also wish to reflect on the following open questions about our sector and the way forward:

- How should the post, parcel and logistics sector position itself and be present in the 'always on' digital world we now all live in?

- What are the essential strengths, unique value propositions and particular expertise that we can bring to our service offerings, and how do we differentiate ourselves in a crowded and competitive market, such as the last mile?

- What is the role of our physical networks and customer touch points in the first and last mile, and how can we leverage these and integrate them into a seamless digital customer experience?

- What are the prospects for parcel volumes and letter volumes as we emerge from the pandemic and, if the significant shift from letters to parcels continues, how does that change our operational focus and business model?

- How do we retain and build our relevance, trust, breadth and reach in the evolving landscape?

- How do we react to the huge global digital platforms that are rapidly swallowing up market share?

- What are the opportunities for more collaboration and partnership with other businesses and organisations to consolidate more, share resources and consume less?

- Where are we finding innovation, fresh thinking and new ideas, and can we provide the platform and/or support for start-ups and small enterprises?

- How are the roles of regulators, stakeholders, owners and governments changing and impacting on our options, opportunities and business decisions?

- How will we emerge from the pandemic? Will we have learnt important lessons and been able to refocus on a more sustainable future trajectory? Will we be more resilient and able to survive future shocks with better business continuity plans in place?

- Finally, what role can we play, as a sector, to show leadership in sustainability initiatives and to use our considerable environmental and business footprint to make a difference globally as a collective effort?

The book is divided into main sections reflecting three broad categories: *Exploring New Directions and Evolving Technologies*; *Navigating the New Digital Landscape* and *Exploring New Frontiers of Business Sustainability*. Each of these categories is further subdivided into specific themes which are briefly outlined below.

OVERVIEW OF THE MAIN THEMES

In the first section, we begin by exploring some strategic directions open to the sector in the context of three key factors which are dominating the business outlook, namely: the long shadow of Covid as we emerge from the global pandemic; the continuing digital transformation taking place and the ubiquity of the digital world; and the considerable challenges of climate change and wider business sustainability.

Several strategic imperatives are identified, including the necessity of understanding the changing market and evolving customer needs, potentially moving further up the e-commerce value chain, and building on core competence in logistics and delivery, bringing to the market unique solutions and service propositions that offer physical outcomes which are fully integrated with a seamless digital experience for consumers and businesses alike. The challenge is to continually innovate and keep pace with technology advances.

There is no doubt that robust digital platforms can enable posts to diversify extensively and forge some very profitable partnerships, as well as remaining nimble, agile and adaptable, providing more and more customer touchpoints across their wide networks, opening up many new market opportunities.

We are reminded that, for business organisations to be successful, it is important for them to understand their DNA and shape their priorities accordingly. The historical mission of posts as a public service was very clear, but this has often become diluted and subsequently confused with the expectations of different stakeholders and ownership models.

Equally, with its reach, brand and trusted reputation, the postal platform is well positioned for diversification into providing wider financial services, which can be done by establishing new partnerships.

At the same time, significant advances in technology are changing many things, from how we live and engage with each other to how businesses and organisations are managed and enabled. Open-platform technology, AI and machine learning are rapidly expanding what is possible. Many of these new developments force us to challenge conventional thinking and allow us to glimpse a future world that is very different to our current experience.

In the tour of relevant new technologies, we are also introduced to the extraordinary power of quantum computing, the use of artificial intelligence and robotic systems to transform parcel sorting, along with a variety of automated vehicles, including drones, self-driving vehicles and autonomous ships.

From facing the disconcerting turbulence of digital disruption, the industry is now rolling back the frontiers by actively exploring the many opportunities presented by this fourth industrial revolution. Navigation is difficult as there are no maps of the future and nobody knows where this will lead, but the journey will definitely be exciting!

In the second section, we have a few signposts and experiences which give some indications of how the sector may be able to navigate and find new territories in the evolving digital landscape.

More intentional and longer-term customer relationship building can be enabled through the better use of data and delivery intelligence, which could transform the market by ensuring the service offering is continually being refreshed and moulded around changing customer needs.

This theme is developed by emphasising the business potential that can be unlocked by adopting an integrated multi-channel approach, based on multiple customer touch points that can give customers what they want, when, where and how, including easy-to-use and convenient self-service options to access services.

However, many of the promised benefits for customer convenience require better and more integrated use of state-of-the-art technology to support interoperable solutions and visibility across the whole value chain. This requires close collaboration across the sector and across country borders, both between traditional posts and with new partners.

The digital transformation of Jordan Post is a good example of what is possible and the kind of difference it can make. This should inspire others to take up the challenge of transforming their organisations and business offerings in order to survive and compete in this new world.

Addressing is a foundation of postal and geographical location services which can also be transformed with an integrated digital approach, as is illustrated here.

Another benefit of going 'fully digital' is to enable significant improvements to throughput, reduce operational risk and lower unit costs, all of which can be powered by the intelligent use of data analytics.

We are also all very familiar with the ever-increasing e-commerce eco-system, which is growing fast to fuel an ever-expanding appetite, particularly for business-to-consumer goods purchased online, that has further accelerated during the pandemic. Fulfilment centres play a pivotal role in the logistics supply chain and they need to be fast, efficient and low cost. Again, this can only be achieved by the intelligent use of data mining, AI and integrated information flows.

For e-commerce consumers, convenience and choice are very important – so what factors drive the choice of out-of-home PUDO locations and how can posts, carriers, PUDO operators and retailers improve the experience for customers?

The third section focuses on all aspects of business sustainability, beginning with a review of green postal products. This covers carbon offsets, sustainable mailing and packaging materials, collecting consumer waste and reusable packaging solutions. What is a greener last mile, and can postal operators supply these kinds of services in a profitable way, at a price the consumer is prepared to pay?

Lower prices, fewer miles and more consolidated PUDO deliveries may be a way that traditional postal operators can still support the USO in rural areas and stay in business, staying competitive. Is this one recipe for achieving business sustainability whilst still being required to offer USO services?

Certainly, the current business context can rightly be described by the acronym 'VUCA': volatility, uncertainty, complexity and ambiguity. So how can business sustainability – resilience, continuity – be ensured in the face of this kind of uncertainty? This presents all kinds of challenges to business leaders, especially how to lead openly and honestly, at the same time as providing a psychologically safe work environment, geared to learning and not blaming!

We return to environmental sustainability with the compelling case for reusable packaging, building on the principle of the circular economy and propelled by the scale of waste induced by the growth of e-commerce relying on single-use packaging.

The increasing demand for last-mile logistics in cities and urban areas brings many challenges including CO_2 emissions, noise, pollution and congestion, but also the need for customer convenience and profitability for the carriers.

This is addressed in different ways, from making a case for customer-focused sustainable business models, to an open-source smart-city concept where the post office can play a pivotal role in its development. To make the last mile truly sustainable may require innovative and ambitiously radical thinking, such as incorporating reverse logistics and even supersonic tunnel delivery.

Sustainability in the last mile is no longer an option but an imperative, and the onus is on all stakeholders to determine what they can do to make it happen.

Finally, consideration is given to regulatory options for underpinning long-term business sustainability. These options will need to cover the evolution of the universal service obligation as it relates to delivery services, and to reflect the changing needs of operators and consumers within the broader industry structure.

The sharp increase in online shopping and parcel deliveries provides particular reasons why regulatory reform needs to be considered with a focus on consumer needs, workers' rights and environmental protection. So, for the last mile it is vitally important that regulation gets the balance right between the competing needs of senders, recipients, operators and society as a whole.

SECTION 1
EXPLORING NEW DIRECTIONS AND EVOLVING TECHNOLOGIES

"posts need to adapt to an increasingly digital world with a constantly evolving service offering"

WHAT DOES THE FUTURE BRING FOR POSTS IN A POST-COVID WORLD?

Holger Winklbauer, CEO
International Post Corporation

INTRODUCTION

All sectors of the economy have been affected by the ongoing COVID-19 pandemic – the postal industry is no exception. However, the pandemic enabled posts to show their resilience and adaptability. The social role played by posts, which have continued to connect citizens and supported their governments by transporting essential medical equipment, has been demonstrated. Furthermore, the COVID-19 crisis accelerated existing trends in the markets and the much-needed postal transformation.

Transit times and service quality were strongly impacted by the COVID-19 pandemic and the lockdown measures imposed in different countries throughout the world. Posts were quick to respond, and prior investment in network capacity and flexibility helped many manage the challenges posed by the crisis.

POSTS QUICKLY IMPLEMENTED NECESSARY MEASURES TO SECURE OPERATIONS

Posts worldwide responded quickly to these challenges, implementing procedures to protect employees and customers while supporting government initiatives to control the pandemic. Meanwhile, close to 60% of posts adjusted retail operations in Q2 2020: reducing opening hours, offering specific hours for priority groups and shutting outlets altogether, either because of staff shortages or government guidelines.[1] Nationwide networks allowed posts to support authorities in keeping citizens informed. Information campaigns were distributed through postal networks and, in some countries, government mail was prioritised. As the pandemic progressed, posts leveraged their networks to offer logistics and delivery for protective equipment and test specimens. Priority and express services were used to ensure fast delivery to labs and clinics. Some posts used 3D printing technology to produce visors and protective equipment for the health and elderly care sectors. Some posts provided welfare checks on behalf of the families of vulnerable and older people. Other posts offered citizens the possibility to send free postcards to isolated relatives during the lockdown.

Despite the disruption, recent IPC research reveals that while in lockdown, close to four-fifths of surveyed consumers were satisfied with the delivery speed of their online orders and noticed little or no disruption to postal services.[2] While most countries were in full lockdown, posts never stopped delivering mail and parcels to citizens. Posts adapted their operations nationally and internationally. Border closures and other transport restrictions also required a shift in operations for posts. While most reported that domestic road transport was unaffected, cross-border operations saw suspensions and delays due to a reduction in global air-freight capacity. By mid-2020, global air-freight capacity was down more than 30% year on year.[3] To address this challenge, IPC helped posts to find alternatives to reduced air-cargo capacity and ensure continuity of international, and especially cross-continental, mail flows.

MARKET DISRUPTION FROM COVID-19 HAS BEEN A CATALYST FOR POSTAL TRANSFORMATION

The COVID-19 pandemic will accelerate postal transformation in the short and medium term. In the immediate future, posts may provide logistics and fulfilment support in the fight against the pandemic, for instance through the delivery of medical equipment and vaccines.

Over the past decade, posts around the world have been facing significant changes in their business, driven by digitisation, e-commerce and new market players. The COVID-19 crisis has reinforced that disruption. The stricter lockdowns accelerated the structural shift from mail to parcels. Mail volume decline has further increased

1   IPC Global Postal Industry Report, November 2020
2   IPC Domestic E-commerce Shopper Survey, September 2020
3   IPC Global Postal Industry Report, November 2020

in Q2 2020, especially for transactional mail, which fell by over 40%. Admail was hardest hit, as businesses delayed or cancelled ad campaigns. Border closures and reduced air-freight capacity saw international mail volumes fall sharply, especially flows from China. Moreover, lower economic activity and pervasive uncertainty saw transactional mail fall by close to one-fifth.[4]

As a result of the pandemic and the consequent lockdowns, consumers have changed their habits and started increasingly purchasing goods online. According to IPC research conducted in May and June 2020, more than half of consumers have bought more online than before the crisis.[5] On average, parcel volumes handled by posts increased by over 40% during the COVID-19 crisis.[6] Posts saw parcel deliveries increase by close to one-fifth on average in H1 2020, though for many, growth was far stronger in Q2. To support growth, posts expanded parcel delivery workforces, with some able to do so by moving staff from declining mail operations.

The overall trend towards more e-commerce and less letter mail is likely to stay. Even if after the crisis the mail volume curves come back partially, they will most probably not be back to the levels seen prior to the crisis. E-commerce volumes will continue growing. This is supported by the IPC research conducted in Q2 2020, which shows that half of consumers surveyed intend to continue shopping more online after the crisis.[7]

CUSTOMER DEMANDS ARE CHANGING TOO

As a result of the pandemic, the purchase of groceries online has increased considerably, and many posts may develop new offerings in that field. Posts will also expect to respond to the increased demand for same-day urban e-commerce parcel delivery.

As more SMEs started selling online because of the various lockdowns and may continue doing so, posts are expected to develop new offerings for SMEs, including consultancy services for SMEs looking to sell online, support with direct-mail campaigns and possible development of online postal marketplaces. Several posts are already supporting SMEs in moving retail online via webshop platforms and marketplaces, as well as access to fulfilment and last-mile delivery services.

---

4   IPC Global Postal Industry Report, November 2020
5   IPC Domestic E-commerce Shopper Survey, September 2020
6   IPC Global Postal Industry Report, November 2020
7   IPC Domestic E-commerce Shopper Survey, September 2020

An accelerated transition towards parcel business will also have operational impacts. Posts will increasingly invest in parcel sorting and delivery automation.

Posts are moving into the highly competitive e-commerce delivery market, especially for cross-border e-commerce, where posts are not only competing with parcel integrators but also with large e-retailer platforms, who are increasingly investing in their own delivery capacities and becoming significant delivery-market players. These large players also tend to offer fully integrated offers both to sellers and to consumers.

To remain competitive in an increasingly crowded delivery market, the postal offer needs to meet three basic criteria:

- The price
- The service quality and delivery speed
- One-stop shop experience for the consumer.

As confirmed by recent surveys,[8] the most important delivery element for consumers is to receive clear information about delivery charges before purchase. The other very important elements that consumers are looking for are real-time tracking, fast delivery, the possibility to re-route parcels while in transit, notification that the parcel is out for delivery, and the possibility to select the delivery company.

This implies that posts need to provide e-commerce customers with full tracking, choice of delivery options and notification throughout the delivery process by email or through an app. While these features are often provided for domestic e-commerce, they can be challenging to put in place for cross-border online purchases. Likewise, providing customers with a full overview of the costs, including possible customs charges – also known as postal delivered duties paid – as already provided by main competitors, is essential for posts to remain competitive in the cross-border e-commerce delivery market.

For posts to meet this challenge, data is essential. Posts need a strong platform to exchange data among themselves to ensure a seamless cross-border flow and give consumers the same range of choices as for domestic e-commerce. Data exchange between posts will also become more and more important to comply with the upcoming security requirements for the import of goods put in place at different levels (US Stop Act, EU ICS2, etc.) and increasingly affecting postal flows.

---

8   IPC Cross-Border E-commerce Shopper Survey, January 2020

Posts failing to offer these features risk seeing customers move away and parcel volumes go down. Utilising their established networks and last-mile experience, and building on close international cooperation, posts can offer a fully integrated e-commerce delivery service at postal rates.

However, the shift towards e-commerce requires a complete change in the offering and the way posts are structured. Infrastructure changes need to be considered and bold decisions taken.

THE TRANSFORMATION CHALLENGE

To successfully address this transformation challenge, posts need to adapt to an increasingly digital world with a constantly evolving service offering. They need to listen to their customers and future customers, and to be ready always to reinvent their service portfolio.

As posts are moving further up the e-commerce value chain, some of them are now operating their own online marketplaces, to create more value for buyers and sellers and to diversify revenue, win parcel volumes and grow their digital brand.

In the competition with large e-retail platforms and e-commerce giants, posts need to think internationally and work closely together with other posts to build a virtual seamless international network. This is one of the cornerstones for posts to win the e-commerce challenge and ensure their place in the market.

CONCLUSION

There are a few prerequisites that posts should put in place:

- Listen to the market to understand the constantly changing consumer, and thus postal customer, needs
- Exchange postal flow data on an item basis between posts to cater for additional e-commerce features
- Offer cross-border e-commerce delivery solutions along market demands
- Facilitate multi-operator agreements
- Share best practices.

IPC is ready to provide this platform for future change.

QUESTIONS FOR THOUGHT AND DISCUSSION

1. *In the huge and fiercely competitive e-commerce market, can postal operators compete across the whole value chain or should they focus on their traditional strengths and expertise, such as last-mile delivery?*

2. *What are some of the ways that postal operators can be more joined up in their operations and data flow, as well as share best practices?*

"The postal sector represents one of the largest and better-connected networks worldwide, and by promoting the synergy between physical and digital channels, it can attract new customers."

THE COVID-19 CRISIS HAS BROKEN DOWN THE BARRIERS BETWEEN DIGITAL AND POSTAL

Stijn Braes, Pierre-Yves Charles and Jack Hamande

BIPT

INTRODUCTION

COVID-19 has changed our consumption habits and Phygital[1] 2.0 has become the new normal in our lives. The health crisis, which significantly limits physical interactions and provoked the temporary closure of non-essential brick-and-mortar stores in many countries,[2] has encouraged the massive use of e-commerce by citizens and sped up the digital transformation movement. People shopped more online and more people shopped online, as e-commerce reached out towards a new clientele. More merchant stores have also developed their approach towards e-commerce. Moreover, online purchases are spread out towards new types of products, with more everyday necessities and items of unusual size or weight.[3] McKinsey even went as far as to state that "we have covered a 'decade in days' in adoption of digital: for online shopping, 10 years in 8 weeks".[4] To further illustrate

---

1   Phygital 1.0 commerce is a physical point of sale which combines the data and methods of the digital world with a view to developing its sales.

2   OECD, E-commerce in the time of COVID-19, http://www.oecd.org/coronavirus/policy-responses/e-commerce-in-the-time-of-covid-19-3a2b78e8 (visited on 16 December 2020)

3   Bpost, the USO provider in Belgium, stated that it was also delivering items like cement during the first period of lockdown in Belgium (*De Standaard*, 4 May 2020, https://www.standaard.be/cnt/dmf20200430_04941196, visited on 16 December 2020).

4   How COVID-19 is changing consumer behaviour now and forever, https://www.mckinsey.com/industries/retail/our-insights/how-covid-19-is-changing-consumer-behavior-now-and-forever (visited on 16 December 2020)

this point, bpost, the USO provider in Belgium, saw an increase in its B2C parcel volume of no less than 79.3% during Q2 2020.[5]

The OECD[6] states that these shifts are very likely to have long-lasting effects, reminding us of the fact that the move of JD.com, now one of the largest online retailers in the world, from brick-and-mortar to online sales in 2004 was a direct response to the SARS crisis. Alibaba's business-to-consumer (B2C) branch, Taobao, was also launched in 2003. Postal services are about to become omnichannel services which endeavour to match what they do physically with what they do online. New services are offered to ensure the delivery of the mail items. The postal sector is at the crossroads of the communication and e-commerce sectors. The crisis has modified users' behaviour by encouraging certain existing practices. Consumers wish to save time and limit health risks. They no longer want a separation between the online and offline worlds. In short, the consumer is no longer multichannel but omnichannel.

MOVING FROM PHYGITAL 1.0 TO PHYGITAL 2.0

Postal operators have been forced to speed up their digital transformation. The health crisis has accelerated development of their new phygital services. This 'phygital' concept refers to all the techniques and processes needed to facilitate the coordination and connection of physical entities and e-commerce activities. These techniques strengthen the relationship between the user and the company. Phygital solutions can also help to reduce points of contact and risks of transmitting the virus in the physical environment. Smartphones can eliminate the need for physical catalogues and bills, by enabling customers to order and pay online. Examples of the most popular services are 'click and collect', which helps consumers buy products online, the 'e-reservation' system, which allows users to reserve a product online, and buy and collect it in the shop later, and 'web to store', which enables consumers to search online before directly buying the identified item in the physical point of sale. TMALL[7] (Alibaba group) and IKEA even go further, by visualising a store during your online shopping trip, so that the complete physical (although still solely visual) aspect of shopping becomes truly digital. These new concepts enable

---

5   Bpost key figures, https://corporate.bpost.be/investors/results-reports-and-presentations/quarterly-results/2020?sc_lang=en (visited on 16 December 2020)

6   OECD, E-commerce in the time of COVID-19, http://www.oecd.org/coronavirus/policy-responses/e-commerce-in-the-time-of-covid-19-3a2b78e8/ (visited on 16 December 2020)

7   Formerly Taobao Mall. The key difference between Tmall and Taobao is that Tmall is a B2C platform but Taobao is C2C.

companies to collect useful information on consumer behaviour via online services. It is vital to allow the mobile interaction of customers with the delivery and other postal services. The potential benefits of digitalisation to connect customers, receivers, operational centres and deliverers have not yet been fully explored and exploited.

The extensive network of points of sale and the number of postmen in the field differentiate the postal sector from other delivery providers. The postal sector represents one of the largest and better-connected networks worldwide, and by promoting the synergy between physical and digital channels, it can attract new customers. Mobile technologies can offer a continuous and personalised customer experience in an omnichannel[8] ecosystem. Phygital is possible in any physical shop, including the post office. Postal organisations must facilitate omnichannel interactions. The postal sector should set strategic priorities and take advantage of its existing assets. The physical postal network represents an advantage for e-commerce. These strategies could speed up the replenishment of stocks and the processing of online orders.

FURTHER DIGITAL INTEGRATION BETWEEN SELLERS AND POSTAL OPERATORS

Robotics is on its way to further bridging the gap between digital and physical with innovations in warehouse logistics, last-mile delivery, stock shelving and so forth. One of the most interesting new offers from postal operators in recent years is fulfilment. This means that e-commerce players can become fully digitally integrated with postal players taking care of 1) goods in, 2) storage, 3) pick and pack, 4) shipment and 5) returns management. The e-commerce players thus never have to deal with the physical products themselves; they become fully digital as sellers. This level of vertical integration can go even further, if postal operators for instance facilitate in creating a webshop[9] – or in the case of bpost in Belgium,[10] even further facilitate the shopping experience by offer a fitting room in the post office, so that clothing can be tried on and, if necessary, immediately returned.

---

8   Relating to a type of retail which integrates the different methods of shopping available to consumers (e.g. online, in a physical shop, or by phone).

9   Bpost example, https://www.bpost.be/fr/envoyer-colis-professionnel/e-commerce (only available in French or Dutch, visited on 16 December 2020)

10 Fitting room in a bpost post office in Ghent, https://www.nieuwsblad.be/cnt/ dmf20181005_03812470 (article only available Dutch, visited on 16 December 2020)

The concept of Phygital 2.0 is the possibility of integrating all the advantages of e-commerce, postal and proximity services in a single experience: you visit your virtual stores and order directly online, your goods are then delivered where you want, and you can enjoy a unique experience at home (or at a local point).

For example, doing an analysis of your body size and shape at a postal point in a 2.0 fitting room allows you to know which size of clothing to choose. The postal point combining local fulfilment capabilities can be used as a key differentiating factor, especially thanks to BOPIS (Buy Online, Pick-up In Store) and BORIS (Buy Online, Return In Store).

BOPIS and BORIS can be illustrated by Walmart, for whom online customer relations are strategic, particularly through the delivery pick-up service directly to the sidewalk. Customers can also benefit from Walmart's shopping drop-off service, which combines the convenience of online shopping with the ease of never leaving the car or home.

In the case of textile products, for example, a customer can benefit from fitting rooms and an advisor ready to handle returns and increase stock. This reduces shipping costs and allows returned items to be put back into inventory in near real time, allowing other customers to purchase the returned products.

The adoption of new technologies such as Augmented Reality (AR) will accelerate this trend. Cosmetic brands like L'Oréal have introduced 'virtual try-on' sessions, where consumers can digitally 'apply' beauty and skincare products onto videos and photos of themselves – even on live videos. Moreover, in China, JD.com will be joining Gucci in offering a mobile AR feature that can measure a user's shoe size via a smartphone equipped with a ToF (Time-of-Flight) distance-measuring camera, which can currently be used to virtually test over 1,000 sneakers on JD.com.

Usually, shoe purchases would be considered 'high touch', as customers would generally want to try them on before the purchase – but these are not usual times, and 'zero-touch' retail is a trending topic now globally.

STRATEGIC DEVELOPMENT OPPORTUNITIES FOR POSTAL SERVICES

The pandemic crisis has forced operators to anticipate the technological developments that will dominate tomorrow's postal landscape. The postal sector is at the crossroads of the communication and e-commerce sectors. The customer relationship must be strengthened. It is necessary to encourage customer proximity and to engage in a relationship of trust. The sector represents one of the largest and better-connected networks worldwide. It is thus well positioned to offer a locally based service. Phygital techniques make it possible to create a unique virtual experience for online consumers. These techniques help particularly strengthen customer proximity and engagement through a relationship of trust, both offline and online.

The phygital postal sector should increase big-data usage, technologies and the analysis of customer signals. The postal sector could also initiate other activities online that are adjacent to its market and adapt its products to customers, by strengthening its ability to work with the leaders of other markets. The mobile follow-up applications of post offices should be evolving to offer new services and features. Phygital should be characterised by the increased use of technologies such as artificial intelligence and an increasing consideration of customer needs.

Customer experience and service personalisation will become smarter and more immersive. High-quality collecting and processing of big data constitutes a sine qua non to obtain an efficient customer experience and instil an image of reliability for users. Tomorrow's online services will be steered by AI algorithms and automated software applications. The postal sector cannot escape this accelerated evolution towards an increasingly data-driven environment. Several postal operators have already developed technologies to process data regarding the perception and preferences of postal (offices') users. Furthermore, new mobile applications have been developed in the field of distribution as well. Where the first generation of applications, 1.0, allowed the consultation of information, in recent years a series of new and more dynamic services have been introduced, such as the postal services related to parcel lockers or track and trace services. A third generation of services, 3.0, should promote interactive content and a personalised offer.

Analysis of consumer behaviour allows brands to improve their customer relationship. Similarly, the recent 'New Retail' concept developed by Alibaba serves as a reference. This entails setting up small commercial spaces, fuelled by online and offline services, logistics and data. In the context of its Tmall Shops network, simple sales outlets become multiservice smart centres, based on e-commerce technologies. Tmall Shops are at the same time supermarkets, post offices, travel agencies and bank offices.

Customers can make purchases there and then, but they can also collect parcels, make online orders or carry out banking transactions. These shops are destined to become actual behavioural observatories. Big-data platforms are rarely conceived to process big data in real time. However, new applications by users and new technologies continuously generate ever-increasing amounts of data. Platforms are therefore encouraged to evolve towards more reactivity and personalisation. The Tmall.com online platform, for instance, provides its users with a unique experience, brought about by the real-time analysis of big data, from the moment of searching until the purchase. The data suggested during the search and the sale are linked to related data and product offers or to marketing material which is continuously updated based on the customer's profile. This model adapts the offer to the needs of the consumer as defined by algorithms.

FUTURE INNOVATION AND EVOLUTION OF DIGITAL APPLICATIONS

At Ericsson Research,[11] the vision is that advanced technology will enable a full internet of senses by 2025 and include the ability to digitally communicate thoughts by 2030. This would mean that simply by 'thinking about having a dinner party', you would already be able to experience the end result. The right music would start to play, the decoration of the room would change, you would even be able to taste and smell the result. Thereafter, availabilities would automatically be checked with your guests and in the end the fresh ingredients would be delivered at home. All without a mouse click or even the use of a touch screen. In the postal field, these innovations could revolutionise the distribution sector.

Interaction is systematically encouraged in order to provide an experience that is as personalised as possible. The user selects the shipping address, chooses the delivery method and can pay easily. Translated to the postal ecosystem, this new commercial model could turn out to be especially promising. Postal operators have a proximity network that is unique in the world and that could constitute a distinct competitive advantage. In the field of Phygital 3.0, postal offices could contribute to serve in 'All In' mode, facilitating the collection of data regarding consumers, whilst contributing to the digitalisation of society and the provision of new online services. Parcel deliverers could offer local deliveries of printed objects, based on 'trade printing', a commercial model allowing the printer to provide brokers, graphic designers, advertising agencies and other companies with printing materials at wholesale prices. This evolution would lead to a re-evaluation of the image that customers now have of postal activities.

---

11 10 Hot Consumer Trends 2030, https://www.ericsson.com/en/reports-and-papers/consumerlab/reports/10-hot-consumer-trends-2030 (visited on 23 December 2020)

In the near future, several innovations will take shape that are related to the operation of colossal data bases, continuously fuelled by the social networks. For instance, the implementation of 6G-related techniques and of connectivity should contribute to the integration of IT elements within the human body. This evolution could enable a direct delivery to the addressee who would be identified and located by means of technological tools within their organism. The notion of signature would have to evolve and make way for a simple real-time identification using the implanted technologies. Other applications and powers could be implanted in the clothes of the postman himself. It is needless to point out that these innovations, which are sometimes designated as 'transhumanism', are controversial. These ideas, which are still in the conceptual phase today, could one day change our perception of the postal sector. The changes brought about by transhumanism and AI are, however, already visible in this domain, in connection with the constant and exponential use of smartphones, applications and smart devices. It is beyond any doubt that the COVID-19 health crisis has been a major catalyst for the acceleration of this evolution.

These technological evolutions must inevitably be considered in regard to the notion of privacy. Article 12 of the United Nations Declaration of Human Rights states: "No one shall be subjected to arbitrary interference with his privacy, family, home or correspondence, nor to attacks upon his honour and reputation. Everyone has the right to the protection of the law against such interference or attacks." Protection of consumer privacy, as laid down in various regulations, is now more than ever a topical issue. The legislators fully understand this, whether it be in Europe, the United States or in Brazil.[12] Consumers are highly sensitive to the matter of privacy. Therefore, the way in which businesses manage consumer data and confidentiality rules may become a genuine competitive advantage. Moreover, in this field, once more, postal operators possess an undeniable advantage thanks to their historic and local establishment. This evolution might also raise questions regarding competition.

CONCLUSION

The COVID-19 crisis has meant that we have moved forward a decade in just weeks regarding e-commerce development. With physical contact strongly reduced and

---

12 Governments have adopted the General Data Protection Regulation (GDPR) in Europe, the California Consumer Privacy Act (CCPA) and the Lei Geral de Proteção de Dados (LGPD) in Brazil.

many brick-and-mortar shops closed, e-commerce reached out to a new clientele, with new sellers and new products. Innovations in AI, AR, robotics and 6G will make it possible to further develop a new phygital world, in which postal operators will become increasingly important as the connector between the digital and the physical. While in terms of innovation the sky does indeed seem to be the limit, other challenges like respect for privacy and competition will probably emerge.

QUESTIONS FOR THOUGHT AND DISCUSSION

1. *There are clearly huge opportunities for the postal sector to exploit its strategic assets of reach, trust and proximity through integrating physical and digital channels into an easy, seamless consumer experience. What are the implications, challenges and risks that come with this approach – and what might be the potential benefits?*

2. *With exciting and futuristic opportunities identified in the phygital world, through innovations in AI, AR, robotics and 6G, should postal operators aim to be at the forefront of these new developments? If so, they may need to be more innovative and less risk averse – how can this cultural evolution happen?*

"The pace of innovation requires planning for the future rather than designing for today, and the economic value to the postal operator is in their network, not within the underlying technologies."

BOUNDARYLESS POSSIBILITIES FOR POSTS

Wayne Haubner, CTO

Escher

INTRODUCTION

My generation has been described as the last generation of kids to play unsupervised in the street and the first to play video games. Growing up during the '70s in rural Kentucky, I remember connecting my Atari console to the family TV and playing *Pong* non-stop with my siblings.

In 1977, the Atari 2600 could perform approximately 0.51 million transactions per second (MIPS).[1] An iPhone 6 circa 2014 can process 25,000 MIPS,[1] while the recent Apple A14 chip powering the iPhone 12 can perform over 11 trillion operations per second.[2] Technology has advanced so much over the past 40 years that we cannot even use a common unit of measurement to describe the speed of innovation. Atari's performance barely registers using the term MIPS, while the term MIPS is a completely obsolete way to describe the processing capability of the A14 chip.

---

1   Console Power Over Time, Liberty Games, https://www.libertygames.co.uk/content/console-power

2   Apple's A14 Packs 134 Million Transistors/mm² but Falls Short of TSMC's Density Claims, 27 October 2020, Semi Analysis, https://semianalysis.com/apples-a14-packs-134-million-transistors-mm2-but-falls-far-short-of-tsmcs-density-claims

WHY DIGITAL STRATEGIES FAIL

Business leaders have difficulty comprehending the staggering speed of digital technology evolution. Even with the past 40 years' experience, executives struggle to imagine the technology capabilities of the future. Many companies' digital strategies fail because their leaders do not recognise how technology advancements will disrupt their businesses.[3]

It is difficult to recognise the impact of technology advancement because human brains prefer to think of the world as a series of linear and incremental steps moving people from their current state to some desired future state. However, advancements in digital capabilities are exponential. Leading scientists, including Gordon Moore, Mark Kryder, George Gilder and Bob Metcalfe, have demonstrated for decades that the foundational technologies of computing, storage, communication and the networks that power our society will continue to grow at an exponential rate.

DIGITAL TRANSFORMATION OF POSTAL OPERATORS

Postal operators have a business model that is hundreds of years old, often predating the countries in which they operate. This business model is built on trust, reliability and a passion for serving their communities. Postal operators have witnessed significant change and disruption to their business model over the centuries.

The changes impacting modern-day postal operators provide a unique opportunity to reimagine their business model. The forces of the global pandemic, climate change and natural disasters, accompanied by social, economic and political unrest, have conspired to create a turbulent world. To address these challenges, postal operators can leverage technology to meet the changing needs of the communities they serve.

The challenges of the global pandemic have accelerated the digital transformation in many industries. Industry leaders such as Microsoft's CEO, Satya Nadella, acknowledge they are now measuring transformation in months instead of years.[4]

The pandemic has also caused parcel volumes to increase 30–50% or more, forcing postal operators to respond quickly to the unexpected volume growth. Postal

---

3   Why Digital Strategies Fail, *McKinsey Quarterly*, January 2018, McKinsey & Company, https://www.mckinsey.com/~/media/McKinsey/Business%20Functions/McKinsey%20Digital/Our%20Insights/Why%20digital%20strategies%20fail/Why-digital-strategies-fail.ashx

4   2 Years of Digital Transformation in 2 Months, https://www.microsoft.com/en-us/microsoft-365/blog/2020/04/30/2-years-digital-transformation-2-months

operators had carefully planned parcel volumes for the next five to ten years, only to have the ten-year volume estimates be realised in just one or two months.

So, what are the implications for postal operators?

What is impossible or difficult today will be possible tomorrow and the capabilities of the underlying technologies will continue to increase exponentially while the cost continues to decrease. Consumers will quickly adopt these capabilities in other industries and simply expect them from postal operators.

The pace of innovation requires planning for the future rather than designing for today, and the economic value to the postal operator is in their network, not within the underlying technologies.

THE NETWORK IS THE ECONOMIC ENGINE OF GROWTH

When we think of current companies that have generated significant value by exploiting the disruption and advancements associated with digital technology, Apple, Amazon, Google and Facebook certainly come to mind. The value of these companies is not in their underlying technology but rather in their networks. If we consider Amazon Web Services as a standalone business, it would be valued at over half a trillion dollars.[5]

Understanding that there is significant economic value to be derived from the network offers an exciting opportunity for postal operators. In almost every country, the postal operator has the largest physical network of retail outlets, distribution, pick-up, drop-off and delivery points within the country. For example, in the United States, there are over 31,000 retail post offices and over 160 million delivery points.[6] In the United States, there are more post offices than McDonald's restaurants.[7]

THE DIGITALISATION OF THE POSTAL NETWORK

While a large physical network is a significant asset to be leveraged in digital transformation, it also creates a significant liability. In many countries, the fixed cost structure of the physical retail and delivery networks is not aligned with the

---

5   Amazon Web Services Is Worth Half a Trillion Dollars, Analyst Estimates, *Barron's*, 28 May 2019, https://www.barrons.com/articles/amazon-stock-web-services-worth-half-a-trillion-dollars-51559060451

6   USPS Facts, United States Postal Service, https://facts.usps.com

7   Number of McDonald's in the United States, https://www.statista.com/statistics/256040/mcdonalds-restaurants-in-north-america

economic realities of the modern world. Research at Escher Group suggests that the operational expense of a small community post office within the network could be $8,000 to $10,000 per year. The operating expense breakdown is 70% of the total allocated to staff, 20% to logistics and 10% to IT and technology.

Postal operators can adapt their networks and services to meet the changing needs of their customers by addressing the following two questions:

1. How do postal operators transform their existing physical networks into a unified network that combines digital and physical endpoints and services to meet the changing needs of their customers?

2. How can the capital and operational costs of the physical network be reduced or eliminated to serve those customers more efficiently and profitably – and with new services?

Postal operators often perceive conflicting priorities of transforming service (or adding new service) and reducing cost. Successful postal operators recognise delivery of new and improved services to their customers as a strategic initiative. Further, they recognise that reducing cost is an operational necessity, but it is not in and of itself a growth strategy.

THE AGILE NETWORK

The postal operator's network is the greatest economic engine to power future growth. How can we transform it into an agile network, providing flexibility to adapt to changing business needs?

An agile network has the following capabilities:

1. *Rapid Scalability* – The ability to expand or contract the number of endpoints to meet fluctuating capacity needs of the network.

2. *Real-time Response* – The ability to respond to changes in real time. The network should have the ability to add endpoints or capabilities within minutes or hours as opposed to the weeks, months or even years traditionally required to facilitate a change.

3. *Thriving Partner Ecosystem* – The ability to foster an open ecosystem of third-party partners, vendors and service providers. Almost every modern technology company that leverages the economic engine of their network has a marketplace or open ecosystem to encourage partners and even their competitors to participate in their network.

4. ***Adapt to the Evolving Customer*** – The ability to adapt to changing customer interactions. The network must respond to how and where the customer requires interaction.

5. ***Learn and Predict*** – The ability to learn and predict based on the data generated from the network. One of the most valuable assets of the network is insight gathered from the data generated by the network.

REALISING THE BENEFIT OF AN AGILE NETWORK

Adopting an agile network has already provided significant benefits to postal operators around the world. The following case studies highlight a few of the benefits that have been realised.

THE FRANCHISE POSTAL RETAIL OUTLETS

A common strategy to reduce the fixed operational cost of postal retail outlets is to transition from corporate-owned, standalone retail post offices to a franchise model where the post office is located within the physical location of another retail outlet such as a grocery, drug or convenience store. The post office can have the same or even greater number of endpoints to serve its customers while reducing the fixed overhead of standalone postal retail outlets. The retailer benefits from additional foot traffic and revenue for their core retail business. The customer benefits from greater convenience and the ability to complete multiple tasks at a single location. Postal operators have experienced lower costs with this model and have also experienced 15–30% growth in their retail postal transactions based on the improved convenience of the combined store format.

SINGLE INTEGRATED POINT OF SALE TERMINAL

Typically, franchise-owned postal retail outlets install dedicated post office counters in the back corners of the retail stores. Some franchise retail outlets are now enhancing their capabilities by integrating the postal transactions directly into the front-of-store commercial point-of-sale terminals. Customers no longer need to stand in two separate lines to conduct postal and traditional retail transactions. Franchise store owners recognise greater flexibility in staffing as one clerk can perform both types of transactions from a single POS device. Providing customers greater accessibility and convenience is a proven strategy to increase revenue for both the postal operator and franchiser.

REAL-TIME DEPLOYMENT OF POSTAL SERVICES

Postal operators can deploy new endpoints or services in their network in a matter of minutes. This capability allows postal operators to establish hundreds of new pick-up and drop-off locations during peak holiday periods. Similarly, postal operators could use this capability to onboard peak-time couriers or delivery personnel to handle any overflow parcel delivery volume. Once the peak has ended, the additional capacity can be deprovisioned as quickly as it was established. Postal operators can benefit by rapidly expanding their network to handle peak volume without incurring any long-term or fixed cost.

MOBILE POSTMAN

Postal operators also have a large number of letter and parcel delivery personnel within their network. Either by foot or vehicle, these delivery personnel reach every delivery point within the network. Previously, we have illustrated that the agile network deploys any postal transaction or service to any location. These services can also be deployed on the handheld device used by delivery personnel. Postal transactions are no longer constrained within the four walls of the post office; the entire capability of the physical post office is now available on the go with existing postal delivery personnel. This provides greater convenience to the customer, resulting in greater adoption of postal services and increased customer loyalty.

CONSUMER MOBILE

In the digital economy, customers expect to interact using a personal mobile device. Banking, shopping and even hailing a ride can all be done with the convenience of the mobile device. The agile network enables customers to initiate postal transactions from their phones just as they would interact with other digital services. Payment of a third-party bill, collecting a pension or a payment from the government, returning a parcel or shipping a parcel can be conducted directly from the consumer's phone. In some cases, such as shipping a parcel, the customer may elect to start the transaction online using their phone and then complete the transaction at the physical post office by scanning the QR code on their mobile device, printing the shipping label and dropping off the parcel. The convenience of mobile postal transactions improves customer loyalty and adoption of services.

CONCLUSION

There is little doubt that the future will continue to deliver rapid change and disruption for postal operators, and with fewer boundaries there are more possibilities for posts. Exponential thinking about technology and the foundation of their agile networks allows postal operators to create an abundant future without constraints. In the words of Alan Kay, the founder of Atari: "The best way to predict the future is to invent it."

QUESTIONS FOR THOUGHT AND DISCUSSION

1. *The huge value of the well-known digital giants lies largely in their networks. What is the potential value of the extensive postal retail and delivery networks, nationally and globally, and how can postal operators begin to leverage these assets?*

2. *Which kind of new services can be offered by posts, building on their strong network, with agile capability and the latest technologies?*

"No organisation or business can 'be the best it can be' unless it understands what is at the very core of its business."

DRIVING FORCE – THE 'DNA' OF STRATEGY

John Acton

DPI

INTRODUCTION

If your objective is to be a highly successful organisation and deliver sustainable growth, then it can be argued that you will need to have a strategy that delivers a significant and consistent point of relevant differentiation – one that offers either unique value or relative value compared to your competition. If you really want to 'change the game' and 'hold all the cards' then it should be a strategy that others will find impossible or difficult to copy or emulate.

This could be called your 'secret sauce' or the defining core of your 'business DNA', your *driving force*. It is the component of the business that is at the very heart of your company or organisation. It is the key determinant behind your direction of travel and the management choices made along the way. More than any other strategic area, your driving force will influence the choices made regarding your products and services, your customers and users, their markets and geographical areas. Without an understanding of their driving force, the senior management team (SMT) may have significant challenges regarding their alignment of thinking. In other words, they will almost certainly be divided and split over the direction of travel and where the priorities are. They will also find it almost impossible to create and deliver a growth strategy to beat the competition.

I have observed many CEOs and senior teams within the logistics and postal world in full flight, trying to finalise their organisations' future growth strategy.

Invariably, this develops into a pitch battle between finance and functional VPs disagreeing about budget levels, timelines and priorities. The CEO frequently takes on the role of arbitrator and peace maker. The only common factor shared in the room is a spreadsheet and the EBIT number in the bottom right corner. This is not strategic thinking; it is budget planning. No organisation or business can 'be the best it can be' unless it understands what is at the very core of its business. What is its business DNA, what is its *driving force*.

TEN STRATEGIC COMPONENTS

All organisations, whether they are state-owned postal authorities, international CEP integrators or agile e-commerce start-ups, have ten key strategic components or areas. Between these areas, management must decide where and how to look for opportunities, prioritise their attention and allocate resources. So, what are these ten strategic components that are present in all organisations?

1. Every company employs **technology or know-how** to a greater or lesser extent.

2. Every company makes use of natural **resources** to one degree or another.

3. Every company combines these within an operational **capacity**...

4. Which is strengthened to a greater or lesser extent with their in-built **capability**...

5. All of which results in the delivery of consistent **services**.

6. Every company uses a certain mix of **marketing and sales methods** to acquire customers.

7. Every company will employ certain **distribution methods** to get these products and services to a customer.

8. Every company sells to a certain class of **customers or end users**...

9. Who in turn reside in certain categories or **market types**.

10. Finally, every company, even not-for-profits, monitors its **size, growth, and profit**.

Figure 1 illustrates all ten.

DRIVING FORCE
THE TEN COMPONENTS

Figure 1. Driving force

In practice, one of these will often dominate the strategic thinking consistently over time. Favouring or leveraging this one area of the business time and again determines how a leadership team chooses opportunities and allocates resources. Simply put, one of these ten strategic areas is the *de facto* engine room: it is the company's DNA, its driving force.

To help illustrate this and explore the driving force principle further, let us examine what each strategic area brings and what it can do to shape a business. I must stress this is very much 'from the outside, looking in' – I would never tell a company or client what their driving force is. Let us look at each strategic area and explore some examples of companies that might select each component as their driving force. The examples I use to illustrate driving force are my perspectives at looking at these organisations from the outside in.

STRATEGY DRIVEN BY *TECHNOLOGY OR KNOW-HOW*

A technology-driven company is rooted in some basic, hard technology, such as chemistry or physics, or soft technology, such as know-how or expertise. It will excel at being able to commercialise its know-how or technology to drive growth and fund further investment in its know-how/technology. Ideally, it will be able to protect its intellectual property (IP). 3M is probably a technology-driven business. For many years, at the very centre of its business model has been its ability to identify breakthrough technology, buy it, protect the IP and then commercialise it by launching product after product. To date, 3M has well over 55,000 products.

Several years ago, UPS clearly repositioned itself from being a distribution-driven business to being a know-how-driven business – obsessing about all things logistics.

STRATEGY DRIVEN BY *RESOURCES*

A company whose entire purpose is centred around the pursuit and exploitation of natural resources such as, for example, oil, gas, ore, gold or lithium – but also people and green energy. Resource-driven businesses will focus significant effort in tracking down new pools of the resource. Equally, they will be experts at converting it into a 'commercial state' to generate income and growth. Isotrol in Spain has for many years pursued a resource-driven strategy in renewable energy. If you are a recruitment business specialising in providing warehouse workers and drivers for the post and parcel sector, then you could be a resource-driven business.

STRATEGY DRIVEN BY OPERATIONAL *CAPACITY*

A company driven by production or operational capacity will almost always have a significant capital entry on its balance sheet. Its entire business depends on the effective utilisation of its assets to generate income. It will often operate 365 days a year and potentially 24/7 if possible. Its strategy is to keep the operation running at or close to capacity, continuously. Examples could be hotel chains, airlines, cruise ships, steel refineries, pulp and paper companies, and commercial printers. Many 3PLs, CEP companies and posts could consider being capacity-driven businesses. At the core of their growth strategy could be the sweating of their operational network assets 24/7, 365 days a year.

STRATEGY DRIVEN BY OPERATIONAL *CAPABILITY*

This is when 'capacity meets know-how'. In other words, a capacity-driven business recognises that, to get an edge over the competition and perhaps change the game, it needs to invest in some know-how to create a sustainable difference. It could be some distinctive capabilities incorporated within its operational process that enables added features to its products that competitors cannot match. As a result of this, the company can now either 'fish in a different pond' for its clients or use the newfound capability to secure more business or to command a higher price. In the CEP world, we can think of many examples where players have introduced some new software or technology to deliver a relatively enhanced last-mile experience. For example, DPD's Predict and Precise services and its App.

STRATEGY DRIVEN BY *SERVICE*

A company pursuing a service-driven strategy will be obsessive about delighting customers and users through the provision of excellent value for money services. Whilst many hotel groups will be capacity-driven businesses, the Four Season group is driven by service. In the logistics, CEP and postal world, if an organisation is looking to take the business to a new level, it could evolve its driving force from distribution or capacity to service. This is what DPD did in 2011.

STRATEGY DRIVEN BY *MARKETING AND SALES METHOD*

This is when a company has a unique or relatively strong marketing and sales platform, process or methodology. It can typically sell a wide variety of products through its platform very effectively. Examples include eBay, Amazon, Herbalife, QVC and Avon. Amazon has lead e-commerce from the front, relentlessly focusing on the buyer's shopping experience. Is Amazon a marketing-and-sales-driven business? Maybe. A case could be argued that its driving force is know-how or even capability. What do you think?

STRATEGY DRIVEN BY *DISTRIBUTION METHOD*

A company driven by distribution method will have a unique or relatively strong or distinctive approach to moving tangible or intangible things from one place to another. It does not necessarily have to own the end-to-end system, but will, for sure, control or strongly influence it. Such a company achieves growth by focusing on the organisation and expansion of the system or network. It can also improve its returns by relentlessly seeking to improve its effectiveness. Examples of distribution-driven businesses might include the integrators, such as FedEx, and many postal authorities. Technology platforms such as Netflix could also be distribution driven.

STRATEGY DRIVEN BY A *CUSTOMER OR USER CLASS*

A company that is driven by a customer or user class has deliberately chosen to restrict its strategy to a describable class of customers or users (people). These customers or users have a 'pulse' and they represent the vast majority of people that the company serves. The company then applies considerable effort to understanding the needs, wants and desires of the chosen customer or user class. The company can then grow by continuously looking for fresh ways to satisfy any unmet needs, wants and desires. For example, a shipping software company might decide to become a user-class-driven business because its best-selling software helps distribution managers in e-commerce and omnichannel retail do their jobs more effectively. It would then obsessively research what else it could sell to these people to make their lives easier – for example, packaging material.

STRATEGY DRIVEN BY *MARKET TYPE* OR CATEGORY

A company that is driven by market category has deliberately decided to limit its strategy to a describable marketplace or market type. The core difference between this strategy and customer and user class is that this is a large grouping of customers/users viewed collectively – for example, e-commerce SMEs. Growth is often achieved through broadening the portfolio of products or market types. Examples might include Lockheed Martin, historically serving the military but for many years also successfully serving the logistics and postal world.

STRATEGY DRIVEN BY *SIZE, GROWTH AND PROFIT*

A company driven by size, growth and profit tends to be a conglomerate of often-unrelated businesses. Its sole focus is to grow a portfolio of business interests. Its expertise is in the leadership and management of this broad range of separate businesses. It will also continuously evolve and improve how it identifies target businesses and acquires them. It will often try to standardise the way senior teams within the portfolio do their reporting. Private equity firms may often choose this as their driving force. Other examples could include Virgin Group, Berkshire Hathaway, GE Capital and Keppel Group.

CONCLUSION

We never tell a client what their driving force is. It is critically important that the leadership team themselves have a wide and deep discussion to explore all the options thoroughly. Deciding what their future driving force is going to be is then arguably the biggest single decision a leadership team takes during their strategic review.

So that is the concept of a driving force – 'it does what it says on the tin'. It is the single most significant strategic area or component that is at the very heart of your business and drives much of your decision making. Until now, this was something the senior team might have been doing subconsciously. By understanding the power of the concept of a driving force and transferring it to a deliberate cornerstone of your strategic approach, it can then become a game changer. Once you decide what your driving force is, it can unlock a whole new layer of critical thinking.

QUESTIONS FOR THOUGHT AND DISCUSSION

1. *What is the driving force of your business, company or organisation? How does that inform your decision making, priorities and allocation of resources?*

2. *Now consider two alternative driving forces – for example, operational capability and customer needs. If you adopted either of these, how would that impact on your decision making, focus and resource allocation for the other one? Is it possible to invoke a combination of them to describe your ethos or business DNA?*

"If you really want to bank on the 'gold' that you are sitting on, do something and do it now!"

POSTAL FINANCIAL SERVICES IN TIMES OF CONTINUOUS (DIGITAL) DISRUPTION

Michel Stuijt

Mozaiq Consultants

INTRODUCTION

Financial services have never been 'top of mind' for the majority of posts. In the current competitive space, where fintechs, money transfer operators, mobile wallet operators and many other players are competing for a part of the market along with the traditional players, it is important that postal institutions consider expanding their portfolio of financial services to enable them to serve their customers better. Ultimately, this will also help to improve the income of postal institutions.

POSTS AND PARTNERS

Many posts have considered financial services a 'nice-to-have' income generator, in addition to their core business. Some posts have made financial services their main business, and done so with success. Most posts have happily embraced the additional foot traffic and transaction income provided by financial services. These services were either offered by posts themselves and were limited to what their tradition, regulation and competition would allow, or were offered by partners who happily made use of the available facilities of posts. However, most of these partners would, over time, slowly build strong customer relationships, causing the traffic and transactions for posts to decline and customers to migrate to other (own) agent locations of the partners.

Posts were, and still are, putting some of their most valuable assets at the disposal of their partners, where these partners themselves could not or would not invest in the granularity of a widespread physical network of offices providing regional and local availability of facilities and resources.

This leads to the simple question: where it concerns the provision of financial services in times of rapid digitalisation, is having a great network of physical offices a blessing or is it becoming a curse?

Digitalisation is omnipresent, especially in financial services. Who needs access to physical locations in times where these services are available 24/7 digitally, with digital money, digital remittances, digital savings, digital wallets, digital card schemes and digital customer services, to name a few?

Where are the incumbent money transfer operators – the so-called 'natural' partners of posts for many years – that were always so keen to make exclusive use of the facilities of posts to reach (and to acquire) their customers?

They all went digital (or so they say), especially during COVID-19, accelerating the trend that had already started some time ago. The pandemic has seen a massive increase in the use of digital payment services which has, in turn, led to an increased demand among consumers for more innovative services.

GOING DIGITAL?

Would it help posts to go digital with financial services now that customers are not using the post offices as much as before and the historical agreements with money transfer operators (MTOs) are rapidly terminated where these MTOs move to providing digital services, causing postal income to decline? It might help in certain cases, and some posts have already successfully introduced digital programs for their financial products and services. But is it the right way for most or for all?

If posts go digital now to provide financial services, they would only be fighting the symptoms of a trend that has already been going on for several years, only to be fast-forwarded by COVID-19. And it would mean a drastic change of strategy and budget for many posts that already struggle financially.

The trend of digitalisation is also being accelerated, causing posts that engage in financial services to run the risk of falling further behind, despite their efforts and investments. In a recent interview, Satya Nadella, CEO of Microsoft, mentioned that "banking and financial services have always been leading technology adopters and coming out of this [COVID-19] crisis, there's going to be more of an acceleration, there's going to be a fair amount of disruption... and all of what needs to happen from a financial services perspective will happen with speed and technology".[1]

WHAT SHOULD POSTS DO?

Instead of trying to keep track of current developments – and adapt or even fight them – an alternative would be to smartly convert and develop services. How can this be done?

By carefully defining a long-term strategy that outlines a true **purpose** (business rationale) of engaging (or continuing to engage) in providing selected financial services.

By developing digital solutions together with carefully selected (true) new **partners** and maintaining a dynamic, professional, non-exclusive partnership program where posts continuously determine which partners are best for them.

By reviving and further developing financial services that are **unique** to posts, for example: savings; and selected payments related to governmental services, bill payments and top-ups of local/regional (mobile) wallets whilst using one of the post greatest assets – TRUST.

But this is not all. Posts should make more use of the activities and services at which they excel and which make them uniquely suited to support and embed financial services.

ACTIVITIES TO COMPLEMENT FINANCIAL SERVICES

There are opportunities for posts in e-commerce that go beyond core logistics. To be a major player in e-commerce, you need to engage in the payment and check-out part – that is the strategic objective. Leveraging the superiority of posts in logistics by focusing on providing e-commerce activities extending to include **all aspects** of the e-commerce value chain is one key to survive. With partners, posts could develop services such as digital check-out facilities, digital payment facilities and digital ways to allow customers to choose their delivery options, connected to the postal logistic back office that is already in place.

Digitalisation allows posts to obtain more information about their customers, get more acquainted with them and become more involved in the **customer's journey**. Utilising the wealth of **data** that is already collected and will come

---

1   Finextra, 7 December 2020

into the possession of posts to improve services and monetise is another huge opportunity. Even more so when using blockchain technology, which is another form of digitalisation that may be leveraged for access to data, and for identification and validation of persons and transactions.

By smartly disposing of certain physical locations and/or regrouping locations to free-up capital, the move to digital can be done without budgetary pressure. In short, the move to digital cannot be done without deciding to say goodbye to some brick-and-mortar facilities that are less and less visited by customers.

ENTREPRENEURIAL SPIRIT AND PARTNERSHIP

To capitalise on opportunities, posts must become more entrepreneurial. They need to speed up their decision making and attract people who have experience in financial services. Many are still government institutions, and the decision-making structure is very slow – too slow to cope with ever-changing conditions.

Posts should also ask themselves if they really want the burden of maintaining licences, registration, compliance programs, ongoing scrutinisation by regulators and the need for expensive competent specialist staff if they want to (continue to) engage in providing financial services. Many, if not all, of these services could be offered by partners in a solid and rewarding cooperation.

There are many types of partnership, such as on technology, sales, product development, innovation and operation. The strategic rationale for partnering can be (a combination of) managing scarcity in experts, increasing time-to-market, acquiring new customers, accessing new technology, improving the digital customer's experience or decreasing operational costs. But partnering only to enjoy a marketing compensation for utilising the post's offices and resources is history!

It is not too late for posts to adapt to the current developments in financial services. However, cooperation with the right partners is key, in combination with providing the right suite of products and services.

CONCLUSION

By embracing selected digital financial services and by smartly including these in the postal product portfolio, posts will be able to truly expand and diversify. To make this happen, posts need to cooperate with new, innovative and true partners. That way, introducing digitalisation can be realised quickly whilst generating a positive cashflow from the start.

My advice to posts – don't sit back. Act – and do it now! Do not think that third parties will step in and save you when things go wrong. If you really want to bank on the 'gold' that you are sitting on, do something and do it now!

- The secret to survival is to diversify – broaden the value chain, adding (more) value.

- Survival for posts is about the ability to change and adapt to changing circumstances.

- The way forward is about closing productive partnerships and cooperation.

- Embrace digitalisation but do it smartly and based upon a well-prepared strategy and roadmap.

Posts are (still) sitting on a pot of gold, but they either do not realise this – or are facing the risk of letting others run away with the gold!

QUESTIONS FOR THOUGHT AND DISCUSSION

1. *What are your opportunities for partnering to meet the challenges of going digital and to exploit the new revenue streams in financial services?*

2. *With so many clear benefits of diversifying into financial services with partners who can bring relevant digital and fintech expertise and investment, why are relatively few posts doing this?*

ROLLING BACK THE FRONTIERS WITH EVOLVING TECHNOLOGIES

"Open architecture that is both hardware- and vendor-independent leads to greater handling efficiency, better use of transport resources and far more flexibility, releasing parcel companies from solutions limited by traditional ways of working."

FIRST PAST THE POST

Richard Hagen

Prime Vision

INTRODUCTION

Within the next five to ten years, we will see a fundamental shift in our industry, one where service users will be able to control their own parcels in transit as part of an open network platform. This scenario provides great contrast to the existing closed network model, where postal and logistics organisations dictate everything between shipment and delivery. The current system is inflexible, limits customer choice and can be wasteful in transport capacity. It must evolve.

We see it all the time: four or five delivery vans turning up at the same delivery address over the course of the day, each one operated by a different company. It's inevitable that legislation and customer demand will soon force the industry to combine or share its efforts, largely to support sustainability initiatives. An integrated delivery network will be better equipped to ensure there is no overcapacity in the system, thus reducing CO_2 emissions.

OPEN-MINDED APPROACH

A big facilitator of the shift to an open network model will be the advent of smart parcel technology, where parcels in effect decide the optimum route and method of transportation. The platform for this technology will have sufficient intelligence to determine the best passageway within pre-set cost and delivery time parameters. We will see exactly the same in terms of last-mile deliveries, be it by van, scooter or cargo bicycle. Mounting environmental pressure on final-mile services means deliveries by cargo bikes are already becoming commonplace in cities around the world.

Sure enough, the solution is not there yet, but major players around the world are already experimenting with intelligent technologies, one of which will emerge to become standard.

When the technology arrives, there will be resistance from traditional forwarding agents, courier companies and logistics operators, who will be far from 'open' to an open network model and reluctant to relinquish the control they currently enjoy. But there will be little choice in the face of legislative and consumer pressure for both the lowest possible cost and lowest possible environmental impact. It will simply become socially unacceptable to have so many different delivery vans covering the same routes. How often do we see two delivery vans run by different operators in the same street at the same time? It's a crazy situation that's adding to congestion and damaging the environment.

The whole of society is becoming more oriented to sharing. We share cars, bikes, tools and so on. Sharing has become an important trend of the twenty-first century and will continue as we move forward. Parcel capacity will become part of this trend, which will be difficult to work against because of the social responsibilities involved. Deliveries have to get smarter.

KEEP AN EYE ON AI

Network capacity will come together in the form of a big-data-enabled online logistics platform that does not yet exist, allowing service users (and the environment) to leverage greater benefit from existing transportation means. Technologies such as artificial intelligence (AI) and deep learning (DL) will be major tools for developing a centralised platform of this nature, facilitating interaction between the platform and various receivers and shippers.

In terms of communication, the advent of 5G (or its successor 6G or some form of satellite-based technology) will expedite an efficient and effective network platform.

With such a system concept, the customer will be in the driving seat, communicating over the internet with the parcel via intelligent technology like an interactive tag, for example. He or she can ask the parcel to find the quickest way to its destination (likely the most expensive), or the cheapest way (probably the slowest). The parcel will then make on-the-fly decisions at each gateway on its journey, to optimise the process. Customers might even be able to make last-minute instructions changes, maybe replacing a home delivery address with an office address due to an urgent meeting request, for example. This option will likely incur a surcharge, but the option will be there, nonetheless.

GOING THE EXTRA MILE

Turning this vision into reality requires the advent of local hubs – 'white label' delivery depots – perhaps one or two for a town with a population size of 25,000, for example, and maybe 20 for a city the size of Amsterdam (population circa one million). These small hubs will typically handle volumes of around 10,000 parcels an hour. After the main volume of parcels arrives in the morning, we envisage that the final-mile delivery journey will take place via a single white-label vehicle (carrier independent) in the morning, and another in the afternoon. This vehicle could be an electric van or cargo bike, for example.

Another interesting concept is that we estimate these smart depots or hubs will be 95% operated by robotics. All kinds of automation and robot arms will be in place for pulling parcels from the arriving delivery vehicle, with various types of tipping mechanisms inside roll cages that will push parcels into a sorting system via a conveyor. For efficiency and ergonomic purposes, the sorting mechanism itself will also be robotics based, while automated mobile robots (AMRs) will scurry around the facility, ultimately leading to a completely unmanned sorting operation.

The flexibility that robots offer for sorting and handling will be highly beneficial in these small depots, where having a large conventional sorting machine would not be practical or cost-effective.

ROBOT WORKERS

Steadily, robots will replace humans in the sorting process as further developments emerge in gripper technology, force control and machine vision. It will become possible to automatically process parcels of any shape or size, an outcome that is already exceedingly close to realisation. Technology can automatically recognise about 80% of the current parcel mix. Today's sorting centres are already moving to adopt solutions of this ilk as they offer far greater flexibility and significantly lower capital investment in comparison with traditional sorting machines. In just one-to-three years, we believe robot arms will be able to autonomously recognise and handle around 96–97% of parcels.

It will soon be possible to have robots fitted with a selection of different gripper sets, not just one, ensuring they can handle all shapes, sizes and weights of parcel in a respectful manner that avoids any potential for damage or contamination. The impact of AI and vision is significant as it's about recognising shapes and dimensions on the spot, and subsequently applying this knowledge to a gentle way of gripping.

Of course, gains in CPU power will be necessary to accommodate the required AI, DL and big-data capabilities. Robots are getting smarter and smarter. When you think about traditional robot arms used in the automotive industry, these are simply programmed mechanisms performing the same task over and over. In contrast, the definition of a next-generation robot is a system capable of making its own decisions (armed with the appropriate vision and intelligence). It will determine the optimum movement routines for itself, rather than follow a programmed path. For an AMR, this will not always mean taking the shortest route, because it will depend on factors such as temporary obstructions and other AMR traffic in the vicinity.

FLEXIBLE FRIENDS

Scalability is another factor in favour of robots as it means a facility can grow in an easy and economical manner to meet rising demand or manage demand fluctuations. What's more, robot testing to ensure optimisation can take place offsite, allowing fast and easy delivery once a new facility is ready. We already see instances of full production coming on stream at newly constructed sites within days. The flexibility that comes with using robots is enormous.

While all of this sounds exciting, it may also appear daunting. After all, a robot is about far more than simply moving a parcel from A to B: it is part of an integrated logistics process with a requirement to access all kinds of databases, back-up systems and predictive maintenance platforms. Data integrity and security are paramount. The robot is a small piece – albeit the most recognisable and eye-catching piece – of an entire operation. Linking these components, databases and computers is where a system integrator can add significant benefit – particularly one that bases its solutions on an open architecture approach, thus avoiding the use of proprietary systems that restrict future expansion and investment decisions.

CONCLUSION

As a business ecosystem, the parcel and logistics industry is evolving fast. A big part of this evolution will be the transition to open platform technology. Open architecture that is both hardware- and vendor-independent leads to greater handling efficiency, better use of transport resources and far more flexibility, releasing parcel companies from solutions limited by traditional ways of working. Central to this trend will be the growing adoption of vision-enabled intelligent robotics inside future-proof sorting hubs. Most importantly of all, the service user will have fingertip control, ensuring that the parcel and logistics processes of the future will no longer be constrained by individual players.

QUESTIONS FOR THOUGHT AND DISCUSSION

1. *An open network platform that allows parcels to travel through a route optimised by price or to reduce environmental impact, whilst also being 'white label' or vendor agnostic, is a very interesting and compelling vision. If the technology is becoming possible to make this a reality, what are some of the main hurdles and how can they be overcome?*

2. *It could be argued that in the scenario described above, the parcel itself and the robot workers can be 'intelligent' and make important decisions; so how does this fit with the needs of the originating shipper or merchant, the wishes of the recipient customer or the responsibility of the logistics provider? Who is responsible for what?*

"Computing power is pivotal for the postal business and quantum computing needs to be well understood"

QUANTUM COMPUTING

João Melo

CTT Portugal Post

INTRODUCTION

Actual computing capacity, all over the world, is the outcome of the technical evolution since the end of the Second World War; but it is also the starting point for another technological leap to properly meet the current challenges to process, with efficiency and efficacy, the growing quantities of generated and/or captured data.

Nowadays, there are different types of computers whose working principle is still the same as it has been since the transistor was invented: they are digital, analogue and hybrid computers (data representation), generic or dedicated (objectives), scientific or commercial (raison d'être) and micro, mini, mainframe and supercomputers (computing power).

When focusing mainly on computers with the greatest computing power, one may select mainframes and supercomputers. Both are big structures, although supercomputers can occupy enormous areas. Both are very expensive, but supercomputers are, by far, much more expensive (and require enormous amounts of energy). Mainframes can support hundreds or thousands of simultaneous users and are able to run, simultaneously, several applications/programs. Supercomputers are largely faster than mainframes and have greater calculus capacity and are usually used to run a certain number of applications, very fast – like weather forecasts, seismic simulations, nuclear research, oil drilling and so forth.

Almost every day, new supercomputers are built and there is fierce competition amongst the most advanced countries.[1]

Nowadays, the most powerful supercomputer in the world is Fugaku (Fujitsu) and is installed at the RIKEN Center for Computational Science (R-CCS) in Kobe, Japan. It has a computing power of 442 petaflops (1 petaflop = 1,000 teraflops, or 1,000,000,000,000,000 FLOPS – floating-point operations per second). Fugaku (USD 999 million) will start to operate around 2021 and will be used by various organisations, scientific and commercial.

Will it be possible to go on building – ad infinitum – more and more powerful supercomputers that are able to process, in useful time, a growing number of highly complex calculations based on bigger and bigger databases?

MOORE'S LAW AND FASTER COMPUTING

In 1965, Gordon Moore (working for Intel) noticed the following: the number of transistors in a dense integrated circuit doubled about every two years and, simultaneously, the manufacturing costs decreased 50%; that is to say, the capacity increased and the costs reduced. This became known as Moore's Law. But this so-called law is showing signs of slowing down. There is a physical limit to the number of transistors one can accommodate per square inch and there is a limit to the speed information can flow between computer components: the speed of light. So, all the computers whose working principle is the same – silicon chips – are not now showing continuous speed growth and cost reduction as Moore's Law predicted.

This is because Moore's Law is not a true law: it was rather an observation and not a prediction.

So, a quest for other computing paradigms, along with the greatest possible refinement of existing ones, was launched, aiming to find out how to reach new heights in computing power: 3D computing, DNA computing and quantum computing, for instance.

3D computing is where chips are placed according to a certain type of 3D structure, instead of a 2D one, which shortens the distance information must travel. This results in more speed and computing power in the same space. 3D chips can be 1,000 times faster than 2D ones.

---

1   To find out how different countries score in terms of supercomputing, see: https://www.top500.org/news

DNA computing uses DNA and molecular biology instead of traditional silicon-based technologies.

Quantum computers are based on quantum mechanics and can perform certain types of operations using much less energy, and are much faster and more efficient than current computers.

QUANTUM MECHANICS

The intention here is to describe some basic quantum mechanics concepts for the sake of a better understanding of the potential importance of this topic for the postal industry.

Classical or Newtonian mechanics is valid for physical systems of great dimensions. Quantum mechanics is valid for physical systems whose dimensions are at the level of atomic particles and/or other particles like photons. Newtonian physics is good enough for describing planet trajectories, how a roller coaster works or how a piano might fall on our heads but is inadequate to address movements of molecules, atoms and protons.

In the realm of quantum mechanics, several basic concepts are present: wave–particle duality (particles are waves and vice-versa), quantic correlations are not local (quantum entanglement), measurement determines reality (there is no such thing as objective reality: reality only exists when one measures it) and all that one can know is probabilities.

When dealing with classical computers, the 'bit' is the smallest unit of information. It can assume either the value 'one' or 'zero' – but never both, simultaneously.[2] In a quantum computer, the 'qubit' is the smallest unit of information.[3]

But the real dramatic difference between bits and qubits is the property that qubits have, known as 'quantum superposition', which makes it possible for a qubit to assume a coherent simultaneous superposition of two states, which is vital for quantum computing. So, a qubit can be 'zero' and 'one' at the same time.

---

2   In a classical computer, how does someone materialise a bit? The value of a bit is usually stored as an electric charge, above (1) or below (0) a certain level, in a memory device (e.g. CMOS – complementary metal oxide semiconductor circuits).

3   How are qubits materialised? A qubit can be, for instance, an electron or a photon. If an electron: it can be '1' when it is up (spin up) and '0' when it is down (spin down). If a photon: vertical polarisation may represent '1' and horizontal polarisation may be '0'.

Another characteristic, which is an interesting application when talking about a 'quantum internet', is the quantum entanglement: the quantum state of a particle cannot be described regardless of the quantum state of other particle(s), even when they are a great distance apart. This was described by Albert Einstein as "spooky action at a distance".

QUANTUM COMPUTING VERSUS CLASSICAL COMPUTING

Having presented the basic principles of quantum mechanics, an example is useful to help us understand how a quantum computer works. One good example is a postal optimisation problem: imagine that one needs to define the shortest and fastest route (starting from a sorting centre) to transport a certain number of objects, using a certain number of vehicles, and to deliver these objects to a certain number of destinations. The classical approach is to build an algorithm that will calculate every and each possible solution, bearing in mind all the givens and variables, objects and vehicles and the possible routes to be chosen to reach all the addressees. Of course, one can complicate this if other variables are introduced such as traffic status, temporarily closed roads, weather conditions and so on. So, it is straightforward to figure out that this optimisation problem will require computing power fast enough to produce something in a useful time, because it needs to calculate all possible options (even if the algorithm is smart enough to previously discard certain combinations that are dead ends) and this can take time. A very, very long time.

In a classical computer, the structural units of information (the bits) end up, after the programming language is converted into 'machine language', as 'zero' and 'one' according to the combination that is being tested by the algorithm. And this happens one combination after the other. First, a certain combination is assumed, then the algorithm calculates the output, and moves to the next one to find out if this is better than the previous one, and so on and so forth. So, only after having tested all the possible combinations will it be possible to select the best one(s).

Classical computers are, therefore, deterministic ones.

Using a quantum computer, qubits may assume 'zero' and 'one' at the same time. How is this possible? Well, the scientists do not know why; what they know is that this is a fact. This makes it possible, with fewer qubits than bits, to reach the result much faster. In fact, technologically, in a quantum computer, things happen as if one had many parallel worlds: each one representing a specific possible option that the algorithm may suggest. Then it is easy to understand that, if we can have all the possible options in front of our eyes simultaneously, instead of having to wait while they pop up one at a time, all you need is to pick the best one from among them all.

However, quantum computers are not error free. Factors such as quantum decoherence and other quantum noise may lead to wrong results. That is why a programme must be run in a quantum computer a few times. But this still takes a tiny fraction of the time that would be needed using a classical computer! The results that are more frequently observed are the ones with the greatest probability of being the right ones – as happens when one does sampling for any other purpose. The more times the program runs, the greater the likelihood that the result(s) more often observed is (are) the good one(s).

Quantum computers are, therefore, probabilistic.

QUANTUM COMPUTERS

One can find, nowadays, three main categories of quantum computers, according to their qubit count. This determines the tasks each one is designed to perform.[4]

A *Quantum Annealer* is the easiest to build and is superior (compared to classical computers) in its ability to factor very large numbers (breaking encryption) and to solve optimisation problems (like analysing route data for mapping applications). Example: D-Wave Systems.

The *Analog Quantum Computer* is where the mainstream is heading now, largely because an Analog Quantum Computer is far faster than today's traditional computers and has incredible computational benefits. This type is more difficult to manufacture, but it holds great promise for solving massive problems in quantum chemistry, material science, quantum dynamics, sampling and optimisation problems. Examples: Google, Microsoft, IBM Q, Rigetti, Honeywell and IonQ.

The *Universal Quantum Computer* is the most complex to build but also the most powerful. It will have more than 100,000 qubits and requires massive amounts of energy to operate. Universal Quantum Computers can be used for secure computing, machine learning, quantum dynamics, optimisation problems, material science and quantum chemistry. They can break encryption even faster than any other form of quantum computer. Examples: IBM is designing a chip for Universal Quantum Computing and also doing a lot of work in this area on both hardware and software.

---

4   This description of the three main types of quantum computer is provided by www.secured2.com.

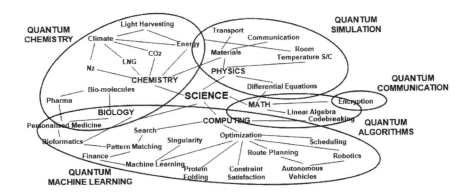

Figure 1. Quantum computing will transform almost every aspect of our technology, science, economy and life

(Sources: World Economic Forum, HSRC, 'Quantum Computing Industry, Technologies & Business Opportunities – 2018–2024' report, industy40marketresearch.com)

CONCLUSION

Having given an overview of quantum computing and its applications, the need to understand its potential future application is clear for any business, including a postal one. It is a fact that every business already is or will be a digital business. Postal activity is still viewed as a labour-force-intensive industry (operations, mailmen, postal shops network, etc.) and it will need to migrate into a scenario, already present but deepening, where automation, robotics, AI, machine learning and computing power are key to competing and survival.

The opportunities for posts that need to be explored rely upon massive capture and processing of data, both from a great many different external sources (e.g. IoPT) and from the objects themselves that are trusted to, handled and delivered by posts (providing that GDPR concerns are properly addressed). Besides, the need to be extremely agile and faster, from the moment any object is received, until it is delivered, requires capacity for processing complex calculations and optimisations rapidly, accurately and in real time.

Computing power is pivotal for the postal business, and quantum computing needs to be well understood – starting, for instance, with scalable pilot projects – so that posts can grasp its full power in due time. It is better to be proactive now rather than reactive later, because failing to understand this may result in a situation like the one that many posts were forced to face when electronic commerce and all its implications 'suddenly' knocked at their door.

QUESTIONS FOR THOUGHT AND DISCUSSION

1. *What could be some of the applications for superfast quantum computing in the postal, parcel and logistics sector?*

2. *With quantum computing, is it important to understand how it works in order to know what it can do?*

"AI tools provide decisions in real time so that the economic benefit can be realised immediately, leading to significant cost savings and much higher asset utilisation."

ADVANCES IN PARCEL OPERATIONS BY UTILISING AI

Dr Thomas Bayer

Siemens Logistics GmbH

INTRODUCTION

'Artificial intelligence' (AI) has been a buzzword since its inception in 1956 trying to mimic human decision making, for example, interpreting images or speech, or playing games. There have been major advances and many successes since then, such as Deep Blue (beating the chess champion in 1997) or AlphaGo in 2016. Not all promises could be fulfilled, however, and there were less successful examples in the past, like the rise and fall of expert systems in the '80s and '90s – difficult to implement by human experts and difficult to maintain.

At Siemens Logistics, we have decades of experience with AI in the field of address reading, from as early as the 1970s. The technology that could recognise and decode typewritten numbers and text on mail pieces for automatic sorting was a significant enabler for postal service providers. Since the 1990s, customers worldwide have been benefitting from software that includes mature machine learning technologies.

Key technologies in AI have been neural networks (NN) along with machine learning (ML). That is teaching computers to do what comes naturally to humans – learn by example. These 'examples' are the key to successful ML applications. A vast number of examples describing the problem space need to be collected, and in addition, all samples need to be verified, meaning that the desired decision outcome needs to be added to each sample. In the example of address reading, each image of a character needs to be verified with its meaning, such as 'a' or 'b'.

For the straightforward application of character recognition, standard NN proved to be sufficient. For more complex patterns, as shown in the subsequent sections, the concept of deep learning is necessary, with multiple layers and much larger structures to be trained.

Simplicity is the beauty of ML – using samples for training the network and then, when good enough, using the network for making decisions. Engineers encountered roadblocks in the early days of AI and ML, in the 1980s or '90s, in terms of available computer power, available software libraries or storage space. Those days are gone and with today's computer power and storage space in the cloud, ML applications can quickly be developed.

POTENTIAL FOR ML IN LOGISTICS

Successful ML applications come with two ingredients: firstly, a well-defined problem space for the decision with a clear business value; and secondly, vast amounts of data representing the problem space. The more constrained the problem space is, the better will be the decision making with a neural network.

When it comes to data, logistics processes generate a huge amount – about shipments, about the network, about the machinery it is processed with and so on. For instance, lots of attributes of parcels are sampled during today's operation, such as size, volume, weight and material (such as soft bag or sturdy box). So, a large amount of relevant data is available.

Also, end-to-end logistics consists of many different processes which are tightly interlinked, from dropping off an item at a centre, across transport, sorting in the hub and delivery in the last mile. Parcel operators strive for the process with the lowest cost position which still serves the Service Level Agreements (SLAs) which the provider promises to its customers. To achieve this, many decisions need to be made to get to the most efficient cost. Hence, there are a magnitude of use cases which cry out for optimisation, for excellent decisions, using ML!

Let us take a closer look at the benefits that AI can bring to parcel handling and start with today's challenges.

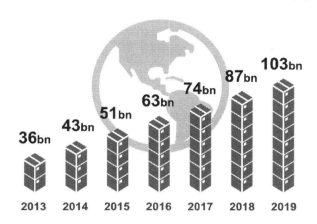

Figure 1. Development of parcel volumes

CHALLENGES OF TODAY'S PARCEL PROCESSING

Parcel volumes have been rising for many years, which has been further accelerated by the pandemic. Reported parcel growth (CAGR) was around 15% over the last six years, according to different studies, leading to a tripling of volumes compared to 2013 (see Figure 1). As a result, some sorting centres are currently overwhelmed with shipments. In recent years, operators talked about peak time in the last quarter of the year; now, peak time is throughout the year!

Thus, maximising asset utilisation of existing sorting hubs is key to cope with the huge loads of today and tomorrow, to sort as many parcels as possible with existing equipment.

Sorting centres are typically designed to process a certain volume of parcels per hour (e.g. 60k p/h). In daily operation, however, the actual throughput might be quite disappointing as nominal capacities are rarely met. Figure 2 gives a snapshot of the actual throughput. The nominal capacity of this sorting centre is 60k per hour, whereas the actual throughput is, at its maximum, 50k – which is 10k short of its capacity!

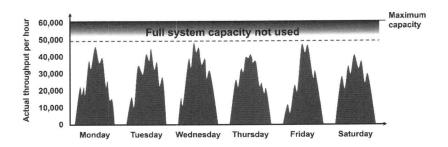

Figure 2. Comparison of nominal vs actual throughput of a sorting centre over time

The reasons for this mismatch can be manifold and complex. They can be network issues, such as: are the volumes assigned in the right way to the network? are transport capacities ok? is the staffing in the hub too low? is certain equipment suddenly failing? and to which degree is the material machinable?

In addition, an important question is how quickly a hub can react to sudden anomalies or fluctuations, for example, a chute for rejects running full, unexpectedly. In times of lower volumes and spare capacity, these anomaly issues were not too critical as the volume to be processed could still be processed in time. In days of continuous peak volume, however, it can take a longer time to identify the root cause of a problem and so, as this can no longer be compensated for in the schedule, capacity is lost, leading to longer and unforeseen production times.

As mentioned previously, logistics operations and parcel operations are well suited to benefit from ML to optimise daily operations automatically – and then make the right decisions by employing the vast amount of data points and learning from them with smart algorithms.

Siemens Logistics has launched different AI software solutions aimed at maximising operational efficiency, such as the Sorter 360, or Hub and Network Booster. Here are some use cases of these products where data sampling, smart algorithms, ML and optimisation tools have contributed to getting closer to the operational optimum and to get the maximum performance out of existing assets.

PREDICTIVE MAINTENANCE – KEEP MACHINES RUNNING

One of the cornerstones of maximising asset utilisation is machine or equipment availability. Parcels can only be sorted if equipment is available and running. If critical technical elements fail to operate properly in a parcel hub (e.g. a sorter fails in the peak period), the sorting centre will lose significant throughput for that period or could stop working altogether.

With the capabilities of the IoT and modern edge and cloud computing, predictive maintenance methods became very popular and useful. With features to predict problems by capturing data from running equipment and using machine learning (ML), a potential failure can be predicted with high accuracy.

Sorters in parcel hubs are operationally critical and so it is crucial for them to be carefully monitored to detect potential failure as early as possible. The Siemens sorter monitoring solution, Sorter 360, with advanced sensors and an edge layer where the captured data is instantly pre-processed and transmitted to the cloud, is designed to deliver this early warning. It fulfils the following main functions:

- Collection and integration of the sensor raw data signals

- Tracking of the carrier position and horizontal and vertical position

- Raw data pre-processing

- Advanced data analytics (running of AI and/or ML models)

- Data transmission for further integration of higher-level systems for advanced operations or maintenance.

Based on a plug-and-play approach, this solution fits different types of sorters with minor adaptations required.

All components that need to be maintained in the near future are visualised with their exact position on an automatically generated sorter illustration. This enables service technicians to do maintenance and repair work whenever and wherever is required.

Hence, by collecting data points in real time and automatically learning how signal response correlates with defects, maintenance can be forecasted. Decision making exactly when it is necessary, in real time!

OPTIMISE PARCEL FLOW IN REAL TIME

Because of the rise in e-commerce, parcel types have changed considerably. For example, many smaller items are now encountered, as well as soft bags containing garments. Also, the way of handling them has changed due to the significant rise of volumes. Processing speeds have increased and higher parcel volumes are now on the machines (for example, bulk processing mode was introduced). Here are a few examples where ML has brought significant improvements introduced by Siemens Logistics.

Small items are not easy to handle with parcel machinery and often lead to operational disruptions. Some may actually be processed more cost-effectively when fed into the letter or flats stream – or even handled manually. Hence, if intercepted at the beginning of the sorting process, these consignments do not then disrupt the subsequent parcel sorting. The same holds true for soft bags. Overall sorting operations are likely to be much smoother if the information is available from the outset that this object is not a box but a soft bag and can thus be treated accordingly.

Another use case is a potential consequence of bulk processing, which typically needs a singulator mechanism that separates a two-dimensional parcel stream into a one-dimensional one where the items are no longer lying side by side, but have defined gaps between them. Although singulation accuracy is quite high, some items may still stick together, so two parcels may incorrectly be considered as one, leading to a costly sorting error.

All these problems can be solved by image analysis using NNs, deep learning and ML techniques. To introduce these smart algorithms, you need cameras to take images of every surface of each and every parcel, to decipher barcodes, 2D codes or addresses. These images can then be used as a representative data set, adding verification information to these images, such as small item, cardboard-box-like parcel or soft bag, single package (the majority). Some images may show two or more shipments sticking together – and the ML algorithm can be trained to deliver the right decision in real time, enabling the sorting system to optimise itself also in real time. In this way, blockages by small items and bags are reduced, leading to higher asset utilisation, and the small parcels can be sorted more cost-effectively in mail sorting centres. Errors by doubles are eliminated.

IMPROVEMENTS IN THE LAST MILE

Last-mile delivery is still the costliest part of end-to-end parcel processing. Today, a range of software tools already supports this process, from planning routes strategically for the next period to real-time support for calculating an optimised route based on actual parcel volumes for a delivery zone. Still, there is more potential for improvements, with smart data analytics, in real time, to further optimise the process.

Analysis of work loads of carriers in a delivery unit over a longer period led to the observation that carriers are unevenly loaded for their routes. For example, consider the case where each carrier is supposed to receive approximately 200 parcels to deliver their route in time, but some carriers receive only 100 items, and some carriers receive 300. The highly loaded carriers may not deliver all of them that day, which will decrease customer satisfaction.

Optimising the load of carriers for a delivery unit has been addressed by Siemens Logistics: based on the data of shipments to be delivered in such a delivery centre, the AI algorithm automatically assigns them to carriers in such a way that each carrier only receives the number of parcels that can be delivered to the receivers in the foreseen time window. Comprehensive data takes key parameters into account to match reality as closely as possible. For example, whether the delivery point is in a high rise, a residential or a commercial area, on a one-way or four-lane road, with or without parking restrictions, with distance between parking and doorstep, with the typical traffic situation at the delivery point, with weather conditions for that day and much more.

Employing this kind of AI algorithm is an excellent example of the economic benefits AI systems can deliver.

CONCLUSION

Software already plays a major role in streamlining the end-to-end parcel process of today. With the opportunity to inexpensively sample a vast amount of data from machines and from process steps, the foundation is there for successful AI algorithms. The examples above show that these tools have made it from theory to practice in operations. Crucially, these AI tools provide decisions in real time so that the economic benefit can be realised immediately, leading to significant cost savings and much higher asset utilisation.

As the technical prerequisites – computer power, storage space, software libraries – are available, these ML algorithms and solutions can be readily implemented. In addition, software architectures today are well advanced, such as cloud native microservice platforms which will host these solutions. This kind of architecture enables steady and continuous software developments, extending solutions and leading to increased efficiencies – step by step.

Logistics is an excellent arena for successful AI and ML applications. There are many process steps that need optimisation, and mass data is available. Siemens Logistics has the expertise to advance these AI and ML applications, leading to a huge optimisation potential – and we are only at the beginning.

QUESTIONS FOR THOUGHT AND DISCUSSION

1. *If AI and ML can optimise machine utilisation, processing and delivery routes in real time, what needs to be in place to ensure these cost efficiencies are realised and not undermined by other inefficiencies caused by workload fluctuations in the operation, such as less-flexible staff costs?*

2. *What other kinds of applications can be envisaged with AI, ML and the vast amount of data being gathered from millions of parcels passing through the operation?*

"AI enables robots to recognise, localise and handle any type of object and thus automate tasks that would be too dangerous, monotonous or otherwise demanding for humans."

THE POWER OF AI FOR INTELLIGENT ROBOTIC SYSTEMS IN POSTAL AUTOMATION

Stefan Berndt

Photoneo

INTRODUCTION

AI (artificial intelligence) enables the automation of a growing number of business processes and postal applications. The scope and pace of smart automation is directly dependent on advancements in AI and, as such, has experienced giant leaps forward in recent years. Combined with powerful 3D machine vision, AI enables robots to recognise, localise and handle any type of object and thus automate tasks that would be too dangerous, monotonous or otherwise demanding for humans.

So, what is meant by AI in postal automation, how does it work, and what possibilities does it open to factories and businesses striving for modernity, innovation and increased productivity? Firstly, let us look at the very beginnings of AI and its gradual development.

FROM THE FIRST ARCHITECTURE TO CONVOLUTIONAL NEURAL NETWORKS

The term 'AI' can represent several machine capabilities and processes – from simple statistics, through decision trees and up to neural networks, such as convolutional neural networks, or even more advanced approaches such as reinforcement learning.

The history of the development of AI witnessed several approaches but neural networks proved to be the most promising and interesting thanks to their ability to generalise.

In the 1990s and early 2000s, neural networks received great attention thanks to the first successful applications of character recognition that included the **reading of handwritten numbers** on bank cheques and letter ZIP codes. These neural networks were trained on a so-called **MNIST dataset** (standing for Modified National Institute of Standards and Technology), which is a collection of handwritten digits from 0 to 9 used in machine learning and machine vision for training image-processing systems. The MNIST dataset served as the basis for benchmarking classification algorithms and is still used today for training and testing purposes.

Figure 1. The MNIST dataset

Though these classical neural networks can learn practically anything, they represent an old, fully connected architecture, and training them requires a lot of time and effort. This is because all the neurons in one layer are fully connected to the neurons in the next layer – which means there are a huge number of parameters to learn, rising with the size of an image. Though the performance of computers has improved over time, it still takes a very long time to train the recognition of even small images.

A turning point in the development of AI was marked by the introduction of convolutional neural networks (CNNs). CNNs are mainly used for analysing visual imagery, including image classification or pattern recognition, and form the backbone of many modern machine vision systems. Another main field of application is natural language processing.

Very loosely speaking, a CNN is inspired by the visual cortex system in the brain. The main idea behind CNNs is not to connect all neurons with one another, as is the case with fully connected networks, but only with neighbouring neurons to create proximity, since neighbouring inputs, such as pixels, carry related information. This means that CNNs can have several layers, and neurons in one layer are only connected to neurons in the next layer that are spatially close to them. This reduces complexity, the number of neurons in the network and, consequently, the number of parameters to learn. Thanks to this, CNNs are faster to train, need fewer samples and can also be applied to larger images.

The term 'convolutional' refers to the filtering process through which CNNs detect patterns. The individual layers *convolve* (i.e. combine) the input and pass the result to the next layer.

The progress in the development of CNNs has also been accelerated by the advancements in graphics processing units (GPUs). Their performance and calculation power have improved immensely over the past few years, opening up new possibilities for training CNNs.

One of the most recognised leaders in the field of AI, often referred to as the 'Godfather of AI', is Geoffrey Hinton. He has a degree in experimental psychology and artificial intelligence. This combination gave him great insight into how to train artificial neural networks.

In 2012, his student Alex Krizhevsky marked another turning point in AI when he created a CNN that was able to mimic the way the human brain recognises objects. The CNN was named the AlexNet and, for the first time in history, enabled a machine to identify objects like a person. This breakthrough popularised convolutional neural networks and opened up a huge range of applications where CNNs could be used.

TRAINING A CONVOLUTIONAL NEURAL NETWORK

In object recognition, it is important that a CNN has a property called 'invariance'. This means that it is invariant to translation, viewpoint, size or illumination, and so is able to interpret input patterns and classify objects regardless of where and how they are placed in an image. To achieve this, a CNN needs to be trained on a number of examples. One of the best practices to increase the amount of relevant data in a dataset is data augmentation.

Augmentation is the practice of modifying input data (i.e. the original image) to generate several other, slightly altered versions of it. Augmentation techniques include horizontal or vertical flipping, rotation, scaling, cropping, moving the image along the X or Y direction, and others.

Training a CNN on altered data makes its neurons immune to such augmentations and prevents it from learning irrelevant patterns. A flipped parrot will thus still be recognised as a parrot.

What comes in useful here is so-called transfer learning. To eliminate the amount of training data, one can use an existing and already trained network and apply some of its filters for the recognition of new kinds of objects. For instance, a network trained for the recognition of dogs can also be used for the recognition of cats by keeping some of its filters and modifying only a certain part of it. This means that the network will adapt to the recognition of cats.

BENEFITS OF MODULAR CONVOLUTIONAL NEURAL NETWORKS

The great value of CNNs lies in their architecture and the fact that individual modules look at single image blocks. The modules do not need to be trained simultaneously and can be easily joined together. Combining these well-trained modules gave rise to complex architectures that can be used for segmentation.

In contrast to the AlexNet, which can only recognise what is in the image, these complex CNNs can do object segmentation and define the object's location in the image.

This modularity makes it possible to use various input channels, which means that if the CNN was used for black and white data, it can also be used for colour data, and if it was used for colour data, it can be extended by depth information. Adding additional information boosts the CNN's performance, which leads to increased accuracy and better recognition of objects and their positions.

FROM OBJECT RECOGNITION TO SMART AUTOMATION SOLUTIONS

Based on the above features and characteristics of convolutional neural networks, Photoneo used CNNs as a basis for its advanced robotic intelligence systems and automation solutions.

Photoneo's CNN works with black and white data, and colour data, as well as depth information. The algorithms are trained on a large dataset of objects and if they come across new types of items, they can quickly generalise (that is, recognise and classify) objects which have not been 'seen' before.

Let us take the concept of a box, for instance. The algorithms were trained on a large dataset of boxes, so they understand that a box has a certain number of faces, edges and vertices. This principle will also work for boxes that the algorithms have not come across before, even squeezed or damaged ones. The greatest value of AI lies in the fact that it can generalise concepts that it was trained on without further retraining.

This enables Photoneo systems to recognise items of various shapes, sizes, colours or materials – a robotic ability used for the localisation and handling of mixed objects (including organic items such as fruit or fish), sorting of parcels, unloading of pallets laden with boxes, and many other industrial applications.

LOCALISATION AND HANDLING OF MIXED OBJECTS

It might also happen that the algorithms come across objects with features that are fundamentally different from those the algorithms were trained on. This might confuse CNN and cause a decrease in its performance. The way to solve this problem is either to prevent it by expecting 'exotic' objects or to have a good retraining system. In the latter case, the performance will be temporarily lower, but the CNN will be retrained to reach full performance quite quickly.

In case a customer needs to pick unusual items or non-commercial products such as industrial components, the CNN can be trained on a specific dataset containing these exotic or unusual items.

When it comes to the realisation of a customer project, the customer receives the CNN for pilot testing and does a feasibility study to ensure that the network can be used for that particular application. This CNN can then be improved and further trained on images from the pilot phase of the project, which will provide greater variability.

THE GREATEST CHALLENGE IN AI-POWERED OBJECT RECOGNITION AND PICKING

The greatest challenge could also be described as the last piece of the puzzle that was missing in the range of pickable objects. This last piece was *bags*.

The difficulty lies in the nature of bags, since they are extremely deformable and can be full of wrinkles, folds and other irregularities. Despite the challenges that bags pose to AI, Photoneo developed a system that can recognise and pick bags, whether they are full, half-empty, coloured, transparent or semi-transparent. This task is often challenging even for the human eye, which may find it difficult to recognise boundaries between bags that are chaotically placed in a container, especially if they are transparent.

However, good recognition and localisation of bags are only part of the precondition for successful object picking. The other part relates to the mechanical side of an application – the robot gripper. The fact that bags are full of folds and wrinkles increases the risk that they will fall off the gripper. This risk can be prevented by using an appropriate vacuum gripper with feedback.

FUTURE DEVELOPMENTS OF AI

Despite significant advancements that have been made in AI in recent years, the field still offers a vast space for new achievements. For instance, so-called *reinforcement learning* receives great attention as it seems to be very promising in suggesting complex movements – for instance, allowing a robot to adjust the position of an item before grasping it.

Reinforcement learning is not only able to cope with object recognition but also with mechanical problems of an application. This means that it not only enables a system to recognise items but also to assess the individual steps of a robot action based on rewards and punishments and 'calculate' the chance of success or failure. In other words, AI algorithms are trained to make a sequence of decisions that will lead to actions maximising the total reward. An example of the power of reinforcement learning is mastering and winning the board game Go.

Despite its immense potential, reinforcement learning is closely linked to the environment it is set in and to the limitations this may pose. For example, the deployed gripper and its functionalities and limitations will always influence a system's overall performance.

AI is the main driver of emerging technologies and its developments will be very dependent on several factors, including market demands, customer expectations, competition and many others.

QUESTIONS FOR THOUGHT AND DISCUSSION

1. *How can intelligent robotics improve operational processes in the postal, parcel and logistics sector?*

2. *What other applications might there be for AI and intelligent learning as described here?*

"We are seeing increasing capital investment in automated delivery technology and a growing willingness to implement solutions such as drones, robotics and self-driving vehicles"

AUTOMATED VEHICLES RESHAPING THE LOGISTICS INDUSTRY IN 2021

Dr Eva Savelsberg, Markus Sekula and Matthew Wittemeier

INFORM

INTRODUCTION

We are seeing increasing capital investment in automated delivery technology and a growing willingness to implement solutions such as drones, robotics and self-driving vehicles, right across the logistics industry.

Labour shortages, Amazon, luxury convenience, 5G technology, the last mile and consumer demand for the free delivery of goods within hours are regular topics of discussion across the logistics industry. Underpinning many of these discussions is also the broader Industry 4.0 topic: the automation of services by robots and AI technologies. In the first volume of this series, *Exploring New Frontiers: Reshaping the Postal Industry*, we contributed a piece titled 'Drones, Robots and Self-driving Vehicles: Reshaping the Logistics Industry' in which we evaluated the potential impact of each of these autonomous delivery technologies and made a few predictions.

Now, three years on from the release of that book, we will look at what has changed around these automated technologies and what the near future might look like for them. Again, for the sake of this discussion, we will continue to focus on three categories of automated vehicles: unmanned aerial vehicles (UAVs, aka drones), land-based small vehicles (robots) and automotive self-driving vehicles (SDV).

DRONES

According to a study from PwC from 2017, the market for drone technology was estimated to reach USD 127 billion (EUR 106 billion) in 2020, not including military uses. A narrower study conducted by Roland Berger, looking at cargo drones for parcel delivery, has estimated that the market for non-military drones was only worth USD 5.5 billion in 2019 and anticipated that this number would increase to about USD 10 billion (EUR 8.4 billion) by 2025. Roland Berger has also issued an interesting case study where it predicts that Berlin could accommodate 1,200 delivery drones that could handle 4 million parcels per year.

In a recent CB Insights report, the use of drones was not just limited to logistics providers, with the list featuring names like Alphabet (Google), IBM, Apple, GE and the BBC, joining the likes of Amazon, FedEx, DHL and UPS, just to name a few.

We could not talk about drone deliveries without bringing up Amazon. They are still the most prevalent drone advocate with tangible commercial services in place. With the first drone delivery in 2017 in the UK, they have seen slow but steady growth in the service since then. In 2020, Amazon was granted FAA approval to deliver packages in the US market. Prime Air offers delivery in 30 minutes or less for packages weighing less than 2.25kg (5 lbs) and within a 24km (15 mile) range of the Washington, D.C. area.

Finally, the UK's Royal Mail announced in December 2020 that it had partnered with drone specialists DronePrep and Skyports to successfully deliver a package to a remote lighthouse on the Isle of Mull. While it is still very early days, this is another example of a post and parcel operator exploring the implementation of the technology. What is particularly interesting is the consortium approach it has adopted, rather than the in-house development approach seen by most operators to date.

Considering the added complication of flight, continuous innovations, developing FAA regulations and implementation costs, drone technology is still progressing slowly. However, as companies continue to tighten their grip on the value and logistics of effectively utilising drones, we will soon see more being deployed. With such a broad spectrum of usage applications available, a future in which drones are performing small- to medium-scale services, like package or pizza deliveries, among others, is no longer a question of 'if' but rather of 'when'. However, this question of 'when' is still subject to significant debate.

German operator DHL announced that its drone parcel-delivery project was "pure research"; GLS sees drone delivery as a "nice PR topic"; while the German government announced that it will create the conditions and regulations to govern commercial drone flights within the next three years. So, while there is not broad consensus on the 'when' of it, drone deliveries are definitely on the radar.

ROBOTS

Robots, on the other hand, seem to have proven themselves on multiple fronts over the past few years, demonstrating far greater possibilities than their aerial counterparts. Since land-based robots are not constrained by the limitations of sustained flight and associated payload weight restrictions, their potential applications are considerably broader. Labour shortages being experienced across the globe are also providing a major opportunity for implementing robotics of all shapes and sizes to support the manufacturing, order fulfilment and warehouse operations of logistics providers around the globe.

Since 2017, we have seen the development of 5G (high-speed, high-reliability mobile networks) and SLAM (simultaneous localisation and mapping) technology along with increasingly sophisticated WMS and OMS (warehouse and order management) systems. Robots can now cooperate with human counterparts to support and optimise functions for order fulfilment and inventory management across a company's manufacturing and distribution portfolio. The data bridge between consumer and retailer has now become seamless, which allows for orders coming in to be optimised and then a robot's path through the warehouse rerouted in real time. In some cases, robots completely take over functions that humans used to complete or alert the human to the next pick (e.g. picking SKUs for order fulfilment, replenishment, etc.) which has allowed for more efficient use of warehouse space.

A few years ago, there was a lot of discussion around the elimination of jobs like the plight of John Henry (i.e. 'man vs. machine'). However, robots seem to have become more of a sidekick, filling in the gaps that were previously subject to human error. According to a study completed by the UC Berkeley Labor Center, displacement of workers will vary across companies experimenting with robotics but will not drastically impact the industry in the short or medium term. In fact, the robots may serve to intensify workers' day-to-day activity since the robots will be optimising workers' activities and routes in the warehouse to fulfil orders more efficiently, resulting in increased worker activity.

The study went on to say that,

> With continued growth in demand, aggregate employment levels in the warehousing industry will likely continue to rise over the next 5 to 10 years. That said, job growth may be tempered by the increased use of labour-saving technologies in e-commerce warehouses in particular, such as autonomous mobile robots, autobaggers and autoboxers, and sensors or RFID tags applied to goods. Honeywell, for example, has developed robotic unloading machines that reduce the offloading time and work in parallel to the role of workers.

Today, a host of parcel-sorting robots exist, including: the Hikrobot, which features a top speed of 3 m/s; the S20 developed by Geek Plus Robotics, which has achieved a benchmark of 10,000 pieces/hour; Amazon's Pegasus, which is purported to improve sorting accuracy by 50%; the t-Sort robotics system from Tompkins Robotics; the 'hive-grid-machine' designed by Ocado; the Flexo robotics system manufactured by GreyOrange; and finally Zippy by Addverb technologies, which performs SKU level sortation at 100% accuracy at a rate of 20,000 sorts/hour. Compared to three years ago when we penned our first piece on robotics, the tide is swelling. Given the increased prevalence of robotics to sort parcels within distribution facilities and not just a focus on the last mile, robots are clearly going to move into sorting centres in the not-too-distant future.

Leading the charge is DHL, which announced last year the expansion of a trial of the Locus Robotics autonomous mobile robots (AMR) where the robots will fulfil up to 80% of the requirements at various US centres. Also making headway here is FedEx, which has turned to robotics solutions within their sortation centres to help with the rise in parcel volumes stemming from the increase in e-commerce.

The logistics robot market is expected to grow with an 18% compound annual growth rate (CAGR), which equates to roughly 485,000 logistics robots expected to be sold in total from 2019 to 2021. In addition to companies buying robots, we are also seeing companies sprouting up, offering 'robots as a service' (RaaS). RaaS is where a company sets up and rents out robots to warehouse operators and manufacturers much like you would lease out commercial vehicles or equipment. This is especially useful for providers that want to adopt robotics when short-handed on labour during seasonal peaks in activity or that simply cannot make the initial investment of purchasing their own.

SELF-DRIVING VEHICLES (SDVS)

Since we last touched on this sector in 2017, there has been an explosion in demand for self-driving cars from consumers, parcel-delivery companies and shippers globally, all wanting to take advantage of this technology. Others believe it will save lives in addition to allowing for deliveries to run more efficiently. We have divided this category into three sub-sections: SDVs (what you will find on the road), automated yard/shuttle trucks (self-driving industrial vehicles you will find in your depot's yard) and autonomous ships (found, well... on the water).

SDVS

Safety is a big driver in the move towards any automated driving technology, SDVs included. In the US, the NHTSA estimate that in 2017 there were approximately 91,000 reported crashes involving tired drivers, which resulted in as many as 50,000 injuries and nearly 800 deaths. They go on to say that "there is broad agreement across the traffic safety, sleep science, and public health communities that this is an underestimate of the impact of drowsy driving."

Skilled-labour shortages are another significant factor leading to a shift to SDVs. The median age of truck drivers continues to rise around the world. In the US, it is now 45 and in Europe, it is 44. Age is only part of the problem. Attracting and training drivers is also a significant challenge. According to a report from the American Trucking Association (ATA), there are more drivers than ever, but in the US, they still fail to meet the demand. In Europe, currently there is a 20% shortage of drivers and this is estimated to double in the coming years.

When you consider that transportation costs can equate to 45–55% of all costs across the supply chain,[1] it is impossible to ignore the difficulty facing the logistics industry. There is a need for reliable and cost-effective solutions. In the US, this may come in the form of lowering federal age restrictions to allow adults aged 18–20 to drive Class 8 motor vehicles. But there remains a huge incentive for companies like Man, Volvo, Sacnia, Daimler and other manufacturers to come up with more technical solutions like SDVs and Platooning. And it is not just suppliers bringing technology to the market. In mid-2019, the US Postal Service started testing autonomous vehicles on runs between Phoenix and Dallas, noting that the move comes as a means to constrain operating costs as much as it is to improve safety and efficiency.

---

1   Liz Dunn and John Vitou, *Labor Availability Challenges in Logistics Real Estate*

At the beginning of 2021, we learned that start-up TuSimple would be deploying tractor trailers that will drive themselves from pick-up to delivery without a human driver onboard. A big feat indeed, but they are not alone. Close to a dozen companies are moving to develop autonomous trucking. To get an edge, TuSimple has partnered with Navistar and UPS and has begun conducting tests in Arizona and Texas, which have included depot-to-depot routes. These runs have currently included a human driver, but the company plans to drop the driver this year.

AUTOMATED YARD/SHUTTLE TRUCKS

Most manufacturers agree that to bring a Level 4 (fully autonomous vehicle) onto public roads is a medium-term goal, and requires continuous refinement and further investments in the technology. The most ambitious timeframe seen to date is to achieve this by 2024. In contrast, the controlled environments of internal yards are the perfect location for autonomous trucks to be introduced more quickly into logistics operations. In fact, internal logistical operations are where the first implementations of automated vehicles took place.

Automated guided vehicles, or AGVs, were introduced to the maritime logistics sector in 1993 at ECT's Delta/Sealand Terminal in Rotterdam, the Netherlands. Since then, many maritime terminals around the world have embraced the technology in their broader transitions towards becoming mostly or fully automated, which in turn has seen the technology improve and the costs reduce. In the past three years, we have seen significant new options come into the market.

In 2019, two major players announced automated yard vehicles, and there are multiple Europe-based projects actively testing the feasibility of these solutions. ZF released its ZF Innovation Truck, capable of handling swap bodies (which complemented its existing Automated Terminal Yard Tracktor), and we were also introduced to the futuristic, fully electric Volvo Vera for more typical trailer handling. Both are purpose-designed for use in manufacturing and distribution yards, and importantly, both come in at a price that will achieve a strong ROI for logistics yard operations. Dachser and the Fraunhofer Institut are testing solutions together in Dortmund, Germany, and the Austrian Post and the Technical University Graz are also working together to test autonomous technologies.

In 2020, we have seen a significant shift in this space with the introduction of both Outrider and Autonomous Solutions Inc bringing robotic, automated yard trucks into the North American market. While it is still early days, both companies are bringing their own approach to the market. Outrider is bringing its own fully autonomous EV yard truck while Autonomous Solutions Inc is more focused on retrofitting existing yard vehicles with the robotics hardware, sensors and intelligence required to drive them autonomously. In Europe, a German start-up, Fernride GmbH, is looking to tackle a similar problem within the EU context.

Regardless of the automated yard truck solution or approach that the industry takes, the underlying requirement for an intelligent, automation-ready yard management system (YMS) cannot be understated. Given the lessons learned in the maritime market over the past two-and-a-half decades, we can confidently say that simple business rule logic and heavily manual systems will not be sufficient to keep a future autonomous fleet functioning at its capacity or most efficiently. In addition, automation of the yard is not simply about implementing automated yard trucks. An automated YMS is also crucial in driving a strong ROI for these future assets. INFORM's Yard Management Systems has been designed from the ground up to meet these requirements and is automation ready today, leveraging AI and optimisation algorithms to ensure the most efficient operations within automated yards.

AUTONOMOUS SHIPS

Most shipping accidents occur because of human error. The *Maritime Journal* said in 2017, "It is estimated that between 75% to 96% of marine accidents can be attributed to human error." As we see with vehicles on land, taking human error out of the equation could improve safety across the board.

The costs of removing wrecks, the impacts on the environment, and liabilities to the crew and other ships are huge, and there are major incentives to streamlining a solution that mitigates the risk that comes with maritime transportation of goods. However, instead of allowing ships to become completely autonomous, there is a consensus that it is likely that they will be more of a hybrid between remote navigation/control as needed and more reliant on sensor arrays positioned throughout each vessel. Each shipper will have, essentially, a traffic control group that will take over a ship when necessary. The crew goes from being on the ship to sitting behind a desktop in an office building somewhere.

CONCLUSION

As we move into the Fourth Industrial Revolution, the promises of automation are everywhere and three years on from our original chapter in the previous book in this series, it seems clear that the traction for robots (within depots) and automated yard trucks (in depot yards) is clearly moving from concept and into reality. It is important for logistics operators to build on learned experience as they move into the field of automation. In this context, INFORM has been working with automated ports for over 25 years and has learned a lot in the process; moreover, it is part of an industry that is still learning how to implement automation well. This knowledge and experience is built into the core of our software solution, Syncrotess. For distribution centres and post and parcel operators, it is a powerful YMS that supports fully automated and semi-automated yards. With a powerful AI engine, this YMS can complement investment in automated hardware with an automated software solution that can also transform yard-handling operations and deliver a powerful ROI.

QUESTIONS FOR THOUGHT AND DISCUSSION

1. *What are the main factors that seem to determine the pace of adoption and wider use of automated vehicles – and are there different factors for drones, robots and self-driving vehicles?*

2. *The author cites a study which says that robots are not eliminating manual labour but can instead "intensify" workers' activities, "resulting in increased worker activity". What impact could this have on human worker roles in fulfilment or sorting centres, for example?*

SECTION 2
NAVIGATING THE NEW DIGITAL LANDSCAPE

DIGITAL TRANSFORMATION PROVIDING A BETTER EXPERIENCE FOR CUSTOMERS

"postal companies need to revisit the way they create customer lifetime value."

DELIVERY INTELLIGENCE AT THE SERVICE OF A BETTER NORMAL

José Ansón, PhD

UPIDO

INTRODUCTION

The postal industry has been significantly disrupted by changes to consumers' online behaviour and parcel waves resulting from COVID-19. Uncertainty about its future is the only consensus. The 'new normal' is increasingly challenging for an industry that was already under pressure in terms of profit margins and letter-post volume declines before COVID-19. What could appear as great news and a silver bullet – the tremendous surge in parcel volumes – can hide greater difficulties of maintaining current postal business sustainability, both from a financial and environmental perspective, despite record B2C parcel volume growth figures achieved in 2020.

KNOWING YOUR CUSTOMERS

To overcome these challenges, postal companies need to revisit the way they create customer lifetime value. In the post-COVID-19 world, delivering parcels is just not enough in consumers' eyes. Postal and parcel services are delivering their life, their most essential choices, their health and their leisure time. They are actually delivering billions of consumers' lifestyles. Consequently, you should know your customer, her lifestyle and track to see if your delivery service is fully matching it instead of just tracking and optimising a delivery process.

Continuously responding to changes in different consumers' lifestyles will define customer centricity in the post-COVID-19 normal. To reach this new and necessary industry milestone, postal and parcel companies must revolutionise the way they engage with their customers – and they have yet to embark on this journey. This new engagement roadmap must rely on massive collaboration between all delivery networks, whilst also being obsessed by the generation of huge experience-driven data and revenue streams.

Failing to integrate customer lives in the provision of their services will increase the likelihood that postal and parcel companies will fail to meet ever-more-demanding consumer expectations. Digital transformation strategies can only succeed if a perfect match between people's lifestyle and postal services is achieved. Do not care just about their parcels but also commit to bringing them the best predictive life insights, given that you are at the heart of post-pandemic consumption behaviour patterns. Any delivery experience must then be aligned with the way people move, work, relax and rest. If you can enable them to move, work, relax and rest better, then they will be happier with each parcel delivery. Encompassing the delivery in the context of a wider life experience is the key to future success. It will renew trust and bring better business outcomes and be truly essential to people's lives. Indeed, a consumer's experience is not over once a parcel is delivered: it is just the beginning of a consumer's next purchase process.

CUSTOMER LIFETIME VALUE AND DELIVERY INTELLIGENCE

If postal operators create greater value and gain more relevance with their customers, then their services need not remain stuck in the transportation of goods only. Creating the best engagement mechanisms around billions of people's lives is critical to their survival. This is no peripheral issue and must be prioritised in terms of postal and logistics innovation. For these life-centric postal services to succeed, delivery intelligence must move quickly to the next level and the way postal organisations communicate with their customers must change radically. This is not an impossible mission. Let us not forget that the very essence of the postal industry has always been around leveraging its communication network so as to engage with its customers. In the twenty-first-century era of machine learning and artificial intelligence, this communication can now reach unprecedented levels of intelligence.

However, today's engagement by postal operators with their customers is still falling short of the levels of intelligence production required to achieve what is necessary to fully understand their customers. Designing the right conversation with them should be the starting point. This conversation requires absolute transparency and comparability. With the COVID-19 crisis, citizens have become used to monitoring the evolution of the pandemic in their country in real time and comparing it to the outcomes in the rest of the world. There has never been such a strong demand for accountability and transparency.

Postal and parcel services will be no exception in consumer mindsets post COVID-19. Starting the post-pandemic conversation requires a total change in the way that these companies handle and share information with their customers. Postal and logistics firms need to communicate on the current state of their network and operations, equally highlighting both successes and failures, and making this information easily accessible to their customers. They should provide them with international comparisons of their operational and customer life-experience performance in real time. There is no shame in acknowledging failures if everything possible is done to tackle network weaknesses. A totally transparent and internationally comparable last mile would initiate the best possible conversation with customers. It will also invite competing networks to start intensively collaborating in their customers' interest. How well a company can join forces with a rival can even result in a competitive advantage in post-COVID-19 economies.

However, the large amount of internal postal transactional data is not sufficient by itself to successfully cope with the current evolution of the e-commerce ecosystem. It is equally important, or even more so, to smartly combine internal big-data sources, such as tracking systems, with external ones, thereby achieving an enriched postal data environment which pictures and reflects customers' lifetime experience so as to serve them better through the most critical events in their life.

An integrated data intelligence framework, which could be enabled for the purpose of gathering the most relevant internal insights from the postal organisation and the most critical external predictions with information about very-fast-changing consumer behaviours and expectations, is needed more than ever before. This would speed up the transition from the current to the future postal business model by relying on the essential communication role of postal services in the twenty-first-century digital economy.

CONCLUSION

Once postal companies have decided to transform their business model and put communication and engagement with people in accordance with their lifestyle at its very heart, well-targeted artificial intelligence could then automate, accelerate and scale up these combined learnings from the internal organisation and its external environment. Such an approach would, in turn, substantially increase the likelihood of successful digital transformation supported by the right technological choices and knowledge.

Finally, this would deliver a better normal for all postal stakeholders, ensuring care, prosperity and resilience for society at large. Let's bring the post back to communication by reshaping the way it engages with its customers!

QUESTIONS FOR THOUGHT AND DISCUSSION

1. *Arguably, the customer relationship in e-commerce belongs to the e-tailers and merchants, with postal companies (and others) simply doing the logistics and last-mile delivery. So, should postal operators extend their reach (and their ambition), as suggested here, to forging deeper customer engagement and lifetime relationships?*

2. *Is it realistic to expect competitors to collaborate and create an integrated data intelligence framework relating to customers' experiences of parcel delivery where all are open to scrutiny about their successes and failures? If so, how might that be established, and relevant information gathered with sufficient independence, credibility, transparency and integrity?*

"As digitisation is transforming retail and logistics services, postal operators have also started a digital journey to transform their postal outlets."

THE DIGITAL JOURNEY FOR POSTAL OUTLETS AND CUSTOMER TOUCHPOINTS

Erwin Lenhardt

T-Systems

INTRODUCTION

Postal outlets are a key component for postal logistics networks, as important touchpoints for private customers. In particular, during COVID-19 lockdowns, when post and parcel services experienced a significant increase in demand, the importance of parcel shops and postal outlets was again underlined for logistic operators serving private consumers.

Like many other enterprises, posts have expanded their digital touchpoint offerings with portals and mobile apps. In fact, the entire postal logistics value chain requires physical interaction, and the ability to provide face-to-face services continues to be an important unique selling point for postal businesses. Thus, postal outlets in combination with digital touchpoints are an important asset for postal operators.

As digitisation is transforming retail and logistics services, postal operators have also started a digital journey to transform their postal outlets. They are making the points of interaction more attractive for customers whilst also reducing their cost of operation and increasing flexibility at the same time.

FROM UNIVERSAL SERVICE OBLIGATION (USO) TO UNLOCKING BUSINESS POTENTIAL OF PRIVATE CUSTOMERS

National postal outlet infrastructures have been a subject of discussion between postal operators and their various regulators for a long time. Regulators have tended to argue in favour of service users for a USO of national post by demanding operators maintain a certain level of outlet coverage and services. Equally, postal operators have been challenged by the increasing cost of maintaining outlets with declining sales volume for regulated postal services. The postal outlet debate has thus been dominated in the past by the 'cost to maintain USO outlet coverage' and the means to reduce outlet coverage and service times.

These challenges have been addressed by postal operators with cost-reduction programmes such as moving to post office franchise/shop-in-shop concepts, adding new retail products and services and/or taking over other social/governmental services to increase revenues for outlet operations. With postal banking, many posts have carved out or sold off their financial service business, while other posts are considering entering postal banking, which will provide new service opportunities for postal outlets.

With the growing e-commerce parcel volumes during the COVID-19 pandemic, parcel operators have found the need to establish a parcel shop network to better serve private customers with parcel pick-ups – as an alternative out-of-home delivery option with drop-off facilities. Postal operators are profiting from this trend as it can provide additional business volume for their existing postal outlet network.

Parallel to these changes, digital technologies are becoming available that make it easier to manage and reduce postal outlet complexity, increase retail productivity and even more strongly integrate postal operators' various interactions and touchpoints with their respective private customers.

INTEGRATED MULTICHANNEL > PRIVATE CUSTOMER RELATIONSHIP > MANAGEMENT RESPONSIBILITY

Thus, the focus for management of postal outlets has changed from pure cost reduction and USP (unique selling point) obligation to a concept of utilising postal outlets as an important means to unlock business potential by increasing customer retention and new revenues with private consumers.

In the scope of this new focus, postal outlets are an important entity through which to integrate postal retail with first- and last-mile logistics and other physical and digital touchpoints – all concentrated on the private customer base. Several operators are responding to this new trend by organisationally integrating their postal outlet and logistics touchpoint systems into one area of responsibility to drive integration and realise synergies.

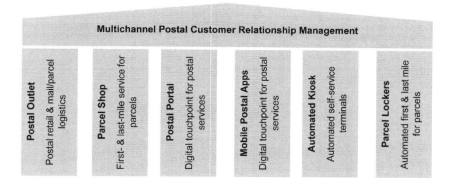

Figure 1. Multichannel customer relationship management at postal operators

As many of the postal retail, first- and last-mile logistics and customer touchpoints are driven by IT solutions, both IT integration and a cohesive IT strategy roadmap play an important role in the successful implementation of this newly integrated responsibility.

STRATEGIES FOR POSTS

Postal outlet and touchpoint developments are closely linked to the latest digital trends in retail, e-commerce and m-commerce, and mail and parcel logistics (postal logistics); and they are also embedded in the demographic changes and shift in customer expectations in this digital age.

However, national postal operators are in a unique selling position with their product mix: they have no direct competitors who can offer a similar mix (although there is competition for some of the portfolio and resources, such as retail manpower and shop locations). Therefore, posts need to closely follow the trends in retail, e-commerce and m-commerce as important guiding signals, but develop their own digital strategy. Figure 2 provides an overview of recent commonly discussed trends in retail, post logistics, e-commerce and m-commerce.

Retail Trends and Priorities	Postal Logistics Trends	E-commerce Trends
• Digital touchpoints will become the first access	• Continued growth in B2C parcel volumes	• Omnichannel integration with retail
• Omnichannel integration	• Optimising parcel returns handling	• Mobile app first
• E-commerce platforms are threat and opportunity	• Continued decline of standard mail volumes	• Reduce % of returns
• Local customer contacts and personal consulting will continue to be important	• Opportunities to leverage trusted brand • Digital and hybrid mail products • Postal retail services • Financial and community services	• Establish physical touch points • Show / unbox / fitting • Click and collect
• Payment and self-service options for customers		
• Digital analytics for shop optimisation		• Digital integration with fulfilment and logistics

Figure 2. Trends in retail, postal logistics and e-commerce

Guided by these trends, posts are developing digital strategies with the following key elements and priorities:

Integration of First- and Last-mile Logistics Information for Private Customers – Most posts are providing information about delivery status and options for their logistics products. They also offer online sales capabilities for purchasing products and provide shop information for postal outlet clerks to service shop-visiting customers (who don't use online sales tools) and also offer more complex services requiring consulting. In many organisations, these systems have been independently developed and they need to be synchronised and integrated, so that complexity reduction and synergies can be realised.

Integrating Digital Touchpoints – As digital touchpoints (portals, mobile apps) have been introduced focused on individual IT applications for various postal products, integration and consolidation are required to reduce complexity, provide one 'touch and feel', centralise access management and improve security aspects.

INCREASING FLEXIBILITY OF SHOP IT INFRASTRUCTURE (SOFTWARE, HARDWARE AND CONNECTIVITY)

More flexibility in setting up and expanding postal outlets requires a highly flexible IT infrastructure (as well as flexible shop outfits). Cloud-based standard retail solutions with API-based plug-in for postal logistics and ERP backends are currently considered state of the art. Shop IT hardware can be fully managed by the cloud solution as well, further reducing maintenance cost. Using mobile IOT connectivity for all shop devices reduces set-up time and increases flexibility to change the shop interior.

'SHOP-IN-SHOP' CONCEPTS AS A DIGITAL ENABLER

Many posts have already moved from managing their own outlet facilities to shop-in-shop concepts. Local retail shops enter into a franchise agreement with postal logistics operators to provide a postal shop within their retail facilities, making it possible to share staff and infrastructure, and cross sell their own products with postal services. This trend continues as postal operators want to maintain and even expand their coverage whilst at the same time reducing costs for shop infrastructure and their own personnel.

With posts digitising their retail services, some operators are also seeking to provide digital services (that are used for the postal IT infrastructure) for use by their shop partner business, making them a digital enabler of small retail businesses. Communication services and cloud-based standard retail solutions as part of the postal outlet IT infrastructure that also allow multi-instance processing can provide such double use of shop IT systems. In this way, one common retail terminal infrastructure can serve as the digital postal front end and as the standard retail front end at the same time. A multi-instance cloud-based retail application can also enable shop owners to manage other retail IT requirements. By providing such services to their shop-in-shop franchise partners, the postal operator can act as a digital enabler for small local shops, providing additional value.

ADDING SELF-SERVE OPTIONS FOR PRIVATE CUSTOMERS

The trend to increase the use of self-serve options for postal services within and outside postal outlets has led to various 'automated machines' being already in use and continues to drive development of suitable solutions for specific postal environments. Solutions range from adding card payment and self-check-out options within shops to automated kiosk solutions combined with parcel lockers in unattended environments. Automated solutions increasingly use central cloud-based IT intelligence in combination with mobile apps, as compared with built-in computing power, to manage simpler electromechanical machines handling the physical tasks of the postal first and last mile.

NEW POSTAL RETAIL PRODUCTS (ANALOGUE, DIGITAL, HYBRID)

As the postal brand continues to provide a trusted image, innovative posts are creating new digital and hybrid products to boost revenues and compensate for declining traditional mail-service revenues. For hybrid products requiring a physical touchpoint in addition to an online service, postal outlets provide excellent opportunities. New hybrid postal products range from ID verification and local community services to making use of postal facilities for e-commerce parcel unboxing and fitting rooms or for 3D printing depots.

ARCHITECTURE FOR A DIGITAL JOURNEY

A digital architecture to allow implementation of the above strategies is typically based on cloud solutions, using standard retail and e-commerce functionalities connected with the postal logistics backend systems via an API-based integration layer. This can enable the deployment of state-of-the-art retail technology and features whilst maintaining the postal logistics and ERP backend on a postal-specific dedicated development track. With rapidly developing IoT connectivity services, mobile connectivity increases the flexibility to add and relocate postal outlets and automated touchpoints.

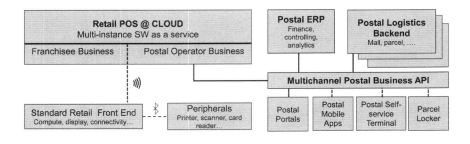

Figure 3. Digital Architecture

THE ROLE OF IT INTEGRATORS FOR THE DIGITAL JOURNEY

A digital architecture and roadmap for postal outlets and touchpoints can include the latest solutions from retail and e-commerce, integrated with postal logistics backend systems. IT integrators with experience of both business areas and familiar with state-of-the-art ICT (information, communication and telecommunications) technology can support postal operators to develop application roadmaps as well as provide the digital infrastructure. By involving such integrators, postal operators can focus on business aspects and requirements while the integrator can take over the handling of technology and technical implementation. T-Systems is active internationally as an integrator and digitalisation partner of corporations and provides end-to-end services.

CONCLUSION

Postal outlets are a key asset to enable postal operators to unlock greater business potential with private customers. They need to be managed as an integrated part of total private-customer relationship management, including other touchpoints such as automated first- and last-mile terminals, portals and mobile postal apps.

Digitalisation of postal outlets is increasingly important for integration with other touchpoints and backend systems, reducing operational costs and increasing flexibility of the shop infrastructure. To achieve this, postal operators need to develop a digital roadmap to continuously improve their IT landscape, aligned with the trends that are driving retail, postal logistics and e-commerce.

Standard digital products which are used for retail operations can be utilised, combined and integrated with postal logistics backend systems. By leveraging standard retail solutions (software and hardware), postal operators can benefit from fast-moving technology developments in the retail and e-commerce areas. IT integrators with experience of both fields – retail and postal logistics – can act as an incubator and accelerator for postal operators to develop and implement the digital roadmap.

QUESTIONS FOR THOUGHT AND DISCUSSION

1. *What are the key factors to consider when reviewing the number and location of postal outlets? How can digital solutions inform these considerations and enable more flexible and agile planning?*

2. *What is the best configuration of physical and digital touchpoints necessary to provide customers with an easy-to-access and seamless experience? Will this be the same for all customers? If not, how can different needs be best met?*

"a seamless supply chain, with the logistics infrastructure blended with current technology, will be the key success factor for the postal industry in the future."

POSTAL SECTOR AT THE CROSSROADS – AN INTEGRATED APPROACH IS IMPERATIVE

Padmagandha Mishra

APPU

INTRODUCTION

Customers are the key to success for any business, and the post is no exception. With the advent of technology and stiff competition in the marketplace, customers are becoming more and more demanding. Customer touchpoints are becoming more crucial for service providers. Last-mile choices are the most powerful way that customers can decide to choose from the options available in the market. In an exceptional time like this pandemic, everyone wants a contactless delivery at their doorstep with up-to-the-minute tracking information at each step. This has posed a challenge for designated operators to have a motivated workforce, combined with the latest technology, ready to perform the delivery service. Further, a seamless supply chain, with the logistics infrastructure blended with current technology, will be the key success factor for the postal industry in the future.

LOGISTICS INFRASTRUCTURE

Modernised logistics infrastructure with innovative shipment solutions and the availability of skilled and semi-skilled workforces will be the most important strength for postal operators in the future. Innovation is going to be the key to attracting customers in the context of changing market dynamics and customer demands. The infrastructure for cross-border logistics relating to leg one (from the point of booking to the office of exchange in the origin country), leg two (transportation from the office of exchange in the origin country to the office of exchange in the destination country) and leg three (from the office of exchange in the destination country to the point of delivery to the addressee) needs to be reinvented. Each leg's efficiency and seamless coordination amongst the three legs will determine the speed and quality of the service offered to the customers.

Again, strong coordination and a good understanding among the different stakeholders of the end-to-end supply chain will decide the degree of success of the business/service provided by the posts of different countries. The stakeholders for international mail services are mainly customs, airlines and the posts/designated operators. Transmission of electronic advance data is one of the crucial factors for the fastest transportation of consignments. Furthermore, it will also ensure the security of the supply chain to a great extent. However, whilst electronic transmission of data is vital, data quality is also going to be a critical deciding factor.

LAST-MILE CHOICES AND QUALITY ENHANCEMENTS

The availability of more options and quality of service at the last mile are vital to the convenience of the customer. Some of the choices may be doorstep delivery and delivery facilities through parcel lockers, placed at post offices, convenience stores and locations near to office buildings, which would help customers get their orders with ease and at their convenience, resulting in minimal contact with postmen or delivery personnel.

Drone delivery in inaccessible areas and for sensitive items like medicines or medical samples is another quality-enhancement measure. Parcel copters can also be an option to deliver parcels to customers in inaccessible and difficult areas, like hilly areas or across rivers, whilst robot delivery has been tried successfully in some countries where the areas to be served are small but accurate delivery must be made.

Postman Mobile Application (PMA): using this application, the postman can deliver different services at the doorstep of customers, such as parcel delivery and cash-on-delivery, and can facilitate different types of financial transactions.

USE OF ARTIFICIAL INTELLIGENCE, AUGMENTED TECHNOLOGY

Artificial intelligence enables computers to perform tasks that usually require human intelligence, such as visual perception, speech recognition, decision making and translation between languages. Application of this kind of cutting-edge technology can make logistic infrastructure truly intelligent and significantly eliminate human errors like missending and misrouting of consignments.

Augmented reality can enable postal operators to highlight specific features of the physical mailing world, increase their understanding of those features, and derive smart and accessible insights that can be applied to real-world mailing applications. Such big data can help companies make more informed decisions and gain greater insight into the mailing habits of customers.

Big-data analysis is also very helpful when considering which type of delivery will suit a particular location, allowing use of the findings to fine tune the quality of the last-mile service.

CONCERN FOR THE ENVIRONMENT AND SUSTAINABILITY

As we know, non-renewable energy sources are depleting rapidly. So, it is necessary to reflect on the available renewable sources of energy to make the entire postal system more sustainable and viable for the future. One example may be the use of electric vehicles by many postal operators for delivering letters and parcels at customers' doorsteps. Many governments provide subsidies for using renewable sources of energy such as solar and wind. The success of this depends on the accessibility and adaptability of such technology. The sooner it is in place, the better it is for the overall longer-term viability of the postal operation.

Some postal operators are already using solar-powered laptops to provide different kinds of services at post offices.

Sustainability is a significant challenge for the post when we think about our tech-savvy future generation. The right mix of people, technology and resources is required for a new paradigm of service delivery.

UNFORESEEN CIRCUMSTANCES

This is also the right time to assess how resilient our postal system is in the face of unforeseen circumstances or conditions like the ongoing pandemic. Are we capable of sustaining our businesses during this kind of major disruption? Is the postal infrastructure versatile enough to face and overcome such situations? Do we have a robust business continuity plan in place to face any kind of disaster, be it a natural calamity or a man-made misadventure? A resilience plan is essential for all the designated operators.

WHAT CHANGES ARE DRIVING THE POSTAL SECTOR?

Traditional systems need to be revamped as the digital landscape evolves and completely changes the business context. Innovation is inevitable.

There are 192 member countries in the UPU, from different geographical regions and at different levels of economic development. For the international postal business to be successful, all postal operators need to respond to the changes together. So, capacity building may be an enormous challenge facing the international postal community. Perhaps a collaboration with private players is one of the available options. In fact, collaboration should be the new norm in place of competition.

One example may be sharing logistics infrastructure by setting up co-distribution centres. Private logistics players have the infrastructure and smart technology to pursue their business in city areas, but they often do not have the last-mile reach that designated operators have. So, a win–win collaboration may be one of the options to consider. It can be approached on a case-by-case basis by different designated operators, depending on their requirements and capabilities, so that the customer at the last mile or at the end of the touchpoint is served equally and efficiently.

Some designated operators are apprehensive about this kind of approach, thinking that collaboration with private players may not be a viable or sustainable option for them in the long run. But with a proper legal framework in place between the two, keeping in mind the strengths and weaknesses of both systems, a win–win scenario could be achieved.

LEADERSHIP DECIDES THE FUTURE OF THE ORGANISATION

It is clear that the postal sector is going through a phase of significant transition and change. During this time, the role of leadership is extremely crucial in the face of inevitable turbulence. So, a visionary leader who can mobilise a motivated workforce with a 'welfare mindset' is more likely to drive the change through smoothly.

Strong employee engagement is absolutely essential, and the desired change cannot be brought about without empowering, involving and engaging employees in the entire change process. Everybody involved in each step of the process, including the postmen who are engaged in last-mile delivery, should be convinced of the utility of new technology in the last mile and its benefit for the organisation as a whole.

FULFILMENT CENTRES

In future, a network of fulfilment centres could constitute the nerve centre of the entire postal supply-chain system. Designated operators are generally the major owners of real estate, and they often have their premises at prime locations in cities. Fulfilment centres equipped with the latest technology may give an edge to the postal operators. These centres could be co-shared with e-commerce companies to assemble, store and segregate both the forward consignments and the return logistics.

Another option is that fulfilment centres could be completely owned, managed and maintained by postal operators, which can manage the orders placed by customers either through their own e-commerce website or through the e-commerce sites of the respective consignors. Sophisticated software and dedicated hardware, along with the provision of real-time monitoring of consignments, blended with their capability to reach the last mile, would give a solid edge to postal operators. Generally, courier companies do not have access to this range of assets and, as such, operate with a limited geographical reach.

REGULATORY ISSUES

Regarding the universal service obligation, all players in the market should equally contribute, as well as operate on a level playing field. Since delivering at the remotest part of their respective countries will not earn profits for designated operators, and since, as a social obligation, it is mandatory to provide the universal postal service to every citizen, all players should take some responsibility and contribute towards it.

HUMAN RESOURCE MANAGEMENT

Skills development is another crucial and necessary step to equip postal employees to cope up with technological changes, social changes and increasing customer demands. Talent management is another important task that must be accomplished by the organisation as market dynamics change and customers want more and more choices every day.

QUALITY OF SERVICE

We may plan to put new things in place to provide customers with adequate choices of service; however, without quality, the desired goal cannot be achieved. Quality must be ensured at each step of the supply chain, right from the booking of the article to its delivery. The concept of total quality management must be ingrained in the system, irrespective of the size of the postal operator. In the process flow, each step is the customer of the previous step; therefore, the target should not just be to provide quality of service at the final stage of delivery or at the booking point, but also to maintain the quality at each intermediate step throughout the process, to get the best outcome.

CONCLUSION

The customer needs convenience. In this competitive and dynamic world, the more convenience a service provider can give to the customer, the more popular it becomes, and the larger the share of the market it gains. A state-of-the-art, technologically empowered infrastructure servicing an end-to-end, uninterrupted supply chain offering an array of choices for last-mile delivery is going to be the key to being a leader in the postal industry in the future.

QUESTIONS FOR THOUGHT AND DISCUSSION

1. *The author maintains that, for the postal sector to survive and thrive, it must embrace new technologies for sector-wide integration and explore collaboration with relevant partners. If this is so, how might it be initiated and coordinated?*

2. *Customers and employees are key stakeholders in this kind of transformation. How can they be meaningfully engaged and involved in the change process?*

"Digital transformation and enabling new services are key for posts if they want to survive and compete."

DIGITAL TRANSFORMATION OF JORDAN POST

Suhair Wraikat

Jordan Post

INTRODUCTION

Digital transformation is no longer a future vision; it has become a key priority as the digital economy is expanding. So, it is not just a project but an ongoing journey of integrating digital solutions into every aspect of business to improve performance and provide value-added services.

This is not only about new technologies but also about business process, changing the way business is conducted, creating new business activities and improving the skills of employees. So, the three pillars of a digital transformation journey are people, process and technology. In addition, innovation is at the heart of all digital transformation.

In the age of digitalisation, postal operators face many challenges. As we see a steady decline in the volume of letters being sent and significant growth in the volume of e-commerce parcels, postal operators must either adapt or die.

Digital transformation and enabling new services are key for posts if they want to survive and compete. Although this is not easy, it offers major benefits and opportunities for postal organisations such as increased productivity, improved customer satisfaction, new revenue streams, reduced costs, higher competitiveness and being able to leverage the post's image as a trusted provider.

THE DIGITAL TRANSFORMATION JOURNEY OF JORDAN POST

The postal service in Jordan is one of the oldest public services in Jordan. The postal network of 270 branches is spread throughout urban and rural areas, offering a wide range of products including mail, parcel and express services, and government and financial services to the whole population. Jordan Post has been focusing on building new business opportunities to ensure its continued relevance and sustainability.

Posts are at a turning point and the postal sector is having to change quickly as emerging technologies such as email, mobile phones and online services become widely used. Consequently, posts need to speed up the digitalisation of their products and services. Jordan Post is certainly no exception in the face of the increasing presence of the digital world. In response, the organisation has diversified into a broad range of new services and is modernising its post office services.

Jordan Post offers online postal services, such as track and trace for postal items, via the Jordan Post website, which has as an artificial intelligence feature, Chatbots, to help customers with their post-related questions. We have developed an interactive platform, JoPost, which is a mobile application covering postal services and new services with increasing levels of convenience, ease of communication and interaction. This includes electronic notifications with pictures of mail and parcels and informed delivery, in addition to subscription services and online postal tariffs. This service also includes provision of virtual mailboxes as the easiest online solution to manage your mail and packages without the need to visit a post office. We are also establishing a comprehensive API strategy to continuously enable new services.

To expand and provide easy access to digital financial and payment services, Jordan Post is an agent of Western Union, MoneyGram, Ria and Urimet. These payment services enable customers to send or transfer money around the world reliably and affordably, and enjoy other creative solutions with instant money services.

Jordan Post also offers the eFAWATEERcom bill-payment services electronic system, which is supported by the Central Bank of Jordan. In Jordan Post branches, this electronic system for online payments allows clients to pay their bills (electricity, water, phone) through flexible payment channels.

The journey from cash to electronic payments also includes encouraging national aid fund beneficiaries to open digital accounts. These can then be used for payments to bank accounts or prepaid cards through which users can receive their monthly salaries, so facilitating the transfer of funds digitally to all beneficiaries as a safe and convenient alternative to cash at post offices.

Digital wallet payments via mobile have been created in collaboration with companies licensed by the Central Bank of Jordan. Jordan Post acts as a white-label agent for all payment service providers through its branches, advocating financial inclusion for the unbanked segment of the Jordanian population.

Jordan Post has also established a joint cooperation agreement with Middle East Payment Services (MEPS). This enables post offices with point-of-sale devices to allow card holders to pay for services available at the post office. Providing these services is in line with the company's mission to support digital transformation and financial inclusion across the kingdom.

A partnership agreement was signed with IrisGuard to offer a service for refugees registered by the UNHCR and the World Food Program (WFP). The registered person is identified on a periodic basis using an iris biometrics scan which is available at post offices and authenticates their identity for payments to support financial inclusion. This improves the lives of Syrian refugees in Jordan, providing individuals and families with a 100% accurate, secure and fraud-proof digital identity in the absence of traditional ID documentation or chip and PIN number cards.

In cooperation with Jordan Customs, Jordan Post activated the electronic Customs Declaration System (CDS). This is one of the technical solutions of the UPU that facilitates the clearance of postal items and parcels so customs formalities can be completed prior to their arrival, thus saving the recipient time and effort.

Supporting e-government, in cooperation with the official government authorities, Jordan Post delivers e-government services output. This enhances collaboration with the public sector, including delivering passport renewal transactions and issuing official certificates with biometric services.

THE FUTURE ROLE OF JORDAN POST – OUR VISION FOR THE FUTURE

Looking ahead, digital transformation will become more important for postal services and consumers. We have only just begun to join the wider digital journey around the world to accelerate business growth and opportunities.

At Jordan Post, pilot projects are underway to provide online transactions at 100 ATM systems, which will be installed gradually, allowing the withdrawal of money using credit and debit cards in post offices. This project will help to establish the necessary infrastructure for electronic payments and provide easy access to financial services.

With our extensive branch network, the company has the potential to meet the needs of customers. Jordan Post will also be partnering with prepaid debit card providers to sell prepaid reloadable cards and gift cards at post offices. These are ideal for everyday use when swiped at a point-of-sale (PoS) terminal or inserted into an ATM, and perfect for in-store and secure online shopping, providing access to physical banking services.

E-commerce is already a big opportunity for us. With our digital transformation, we try to attract parcel delivery by working with shipping platforms to increase the number of service options for online senders. We will also be launching a shipping website for e-commerce fulfilment called myjobox.jo. This will provide a shipping mail address in the US and the UK for Jordanian customers so they can buy products from US and UK brands (shopping online) and then have them shipped to Jordan at competitive rates with tracked packages.

Jordan Post also intends to launch a brand-new e-commerce platform (E-Shop) geared particularly towards stamp collectors, for the sale of stamps, booklets, postcards and collectibles.

CONCLUSION

Going forward, the digital vision and strategy sit at the top of our company transformation pyramid. Development is a continuous process, and we are continuing to respond to wider developments in the postal sector. Going digital is at the core of our business transformation, as our future depends on embracing digital transformation and diversification of postal services. By focusing on the e-commerce sector, we hope to save our postal service.

The future vision of Jordan Post is to become the most trusted company for delivering traditional and digital services with high quality and affordability in Jordan.

QUESTIONS FOR THOUGHT AND DISCUSSION

1. *Technology partners are key enablers for Jordan Post in its digital transformation journey. What are the most important things to consider when selecting a technology partner?*

2. *Alongside the adoption of new technologies, to be successful this kind of digital transformation also requires a complete change in the mindset and culture of an organisation. What does this involve and how do you make it happen?*

"Postal operators can lead the next generation of transformation by adopting integrated digital solutions."

THE BENEFITS OF INTEGRATING DIGITAL TECHNOLOGY FOR SHIPPING AND LOGISTICS

Santosh Gopal

Ship2MyID

INTRODUCTION

It is often difficult to recognise a problem when you've lived your entire life not knowing that a better solution is possible. Bank cheques and money transfers were available for hundreds of years but then PayPal came and disrupted money transfers. Uber, just like PayPal, revolutionised an industry and gave consumers the power to choose how they want things to be done – these companies realise that we live in a digital age and certain 'traditional' business models must be changed to benefit the consumer. Limousine and taxi services were available for a long time but then Uber revolutionised personal transportation by providing more convenience for customers and new financial opportunities for millions of part-time drivers. Similarly, Airbnb disrupted the hotel sector and provided extra income to millions of homeowners who had excess space. Here we will explain how integrating digital and physical identities will disrupt businesses in shipping and logistics, identity management, e-commerce, privacy management, direct mail and marketing, while most importantly creating new revenue opportunities that were not possible before.

HOW THE IDEA BEGAN

Generation Z, which was never exposed to the pre-internet era, carries less baggage from living in the past. Fortunately, they don't take rules for granted and do question the norm. For Kush Santosh, my son and co-inventor of this disruptive patented approach, the journey of realising that there is an opportunity for change in the world of shipping and logistics started when he was just seven years old.

In America, it is customary to offer a token of appreciation known as a 'goodie bag' to guests attending your birthday celebration. On his seventh birthday, Kush encountered a problem when the goodie bags were forgotten at home. In an effort to distribute these thoughtful tokens of good will, the natural option was to send them to the kids' home addresses. When Kush asked his school to provide all the addresses, the administration refused, stating two reasons: privacy concerns, and the fact that the school wasn't sure if the addresses were *accurate*! Instead, they gave Kush email addresses. For the same birthday, I had purchased a Google tablet online that was to be shipped to our house in California. However, the day after I ordered this, Kush was to leave for a family trip to Washington, D.C. Two days later, Google sent an 'email alert' to Kush's email, mentioning the delivery of the tablet to our California address.

These two stories led Kush to ponder – why can't we ship to an email address and why can't the package follow people rather than being tied to a fixed location?

ADDRESSES

Addresses are defined as the geographical particulars of the place where someone lives, or an organisation is situated. Addresses are core to industries like shipping and logistics. They also happen to be central to people's identity. The conventional 'address' has several limitations. Almost every country has its own way of addressing that could include street number, street name, city, county or district, state or province, and so forth. Even the format of postcode or ZIP code is different. Multiple languages make it even harder to decode the address. According to the UPU, in several countries more than half the people do not have structured addresses. Not having a structured home address results in consumers not being able to easily access basic services like insurance, utilities and health benefits. According to the USPS, millennials change address every three years. This means that in three years, your address database will become obsolete. Change of address is the leading reason why people lose their deliveries, especially if the sender doesn't have an updated address.

In the last decade, cell phones have become the medium to connect with everyone in the world. An average millennial may store more than 1,000 digital contacts that could include social-media contacts, cell-phone numbers and emails. However, they rarely store addresses. Equally, having an address doesn't guarantee the accuracy and currency of that address. Data privacy has become very important for the safety of people. Digital life brings a layer of privacy and anonymity, whereas sharing an address is a risk to privacy. We love to have 10,000 followers on Twitter or Instagram applications, but we don't want anyone to follow us in real life.

Several attempts have been made to digitise addresses by linking GIS (geographical information systems), where a physical location is mapped by unique longitude and latitude and then represented by an alphanumeric code. For example, Plus Code from Google or What3Words can represent a three-metre square of the world with three random English words to create a unique and easy way to represent a physical address. Their solutions were simple and removed the language barrier or the need for a structured address, but still fell short when it came to handling changes of address and uniqueness to an individual. Privacy remained a big concern as reverse lookups were public. Knowing someone's digital code would expose their physical address.

Despite rapid technological advancement, our postal system has remained the same for centuries – without an address, there can be no shipment or delivery. The ability to receive packages should not be dependent on providing a delivery address right before the transaction occurs.

We looked at these challenges, reviewed Kush's questions and took a further step to create a patented platform like PayPal, but for *shipping*. We added several other features to this platform that we believe can address most of the problems discussed above and can also create new revenue streams not possible before.

SHIP2MYID PLATFORM – INTEGRATING DIGITAL AND PHYSICAL IDENTITIES

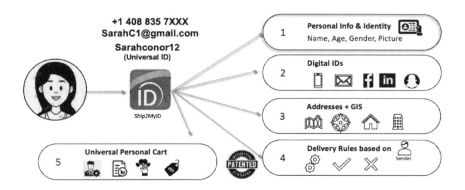

Figure 1

The core principle of the platform is to give control to the consumer. As shown in Figure 1, the consumer can create their own username and link several pieces of their information, including: *personal information* – name, gender, age and picture; *digital IDs* – email, cell phone, Instagram, Facebook, LinkedIn or any social ID; *physical addresses* – the consumer can stand in front of their main door and click a button to automatically capture their GIS and address, or they can simply type it in. They can create several delivery addresses and can also include specific delivery instructions. The platform also provides a *Universal Cart*. This allows consumers to add their personal profile, lists of items recently purchased, wish lists, discount codes and so forth. Basically, this is where a consumer can create their own digital twin. Each consumer can control what information needs to be shared to other parties per transaction. *Privacy Rules* – users have 100% control to manage their privacy and delivery preferences. Privacy is related to our trust with the other parties. The platform lets the consumer choose to accept or not, and where to deliver based on who the sender is. These rules let them manage their entire privacy. Privacy and protection are central to this platform.

Some key characteristics of this NextGen addressing platform include: a unique, potentially lifetime address for every citizen in the world; higher accuracy, as GIS is tagged to each address; ease of use whilst maintaining privacy, with no reverse look up; and the removal of the language barrier and the problem of differing address formats. It is truly global, portable and linked to identities. With this platform, it is thus possible to enable every contact to become a delivery address.

The platform would work well if adopted by one organisation per country, which would then be the custodian of the platform and the data in that region. This organisation would then work with the rest of the ecosystem players to offer the service as a 'single source of truth'. Postal operators in each country would be a suitable entity to own and manage this platform. It would help to resolve data inconsistencies and make it easy for consumers to maintain their information in just one system.

BENEFITS OF THIS KIND OF PLATFORM FOR CONSUMERS

Addressing the Unaddressed – People who may not have a structured address, who are homeless or who live in completely unaddressed areas can be given a unique digital address that can be used for accepting deliveries. In certain countries, their government ID can be linked to this account as well.

Change of Address – When a recipient changes address, they go to the front door of their new location and click a button. That becomes the new delivery address. As senders will always send the packages to a unique digital ID, they don't need to worry about any recipient's change in address or keeping their address database up to date.

Privacy – A recipient address is NOT needed by the sender to enable shipping. So, the sender would never know where the recipient lives. Only the post office, delivery company or custodian of the platform will know the physical location. Consumers and recipients can control what data is shared with others involved in the transaction.

Social Commerce – Social IDs can be tagged to a physical address and consumers can simply ship products to others using social IDs. Through seamless integration, the need for delivery addresses is eliminated. Consumers can also checkout from retail stores simply with their social IDs.

Universal Login – Instead of registering with hundreds of e-commerce platforms, businesses and government organisations globally, consumers are empowered by managing *one* unique global login, secured with multi-factor authentication. The less data 'out there', the better it is for privacy. This would significantly reduce data inconsistency and fraud activities.

BENEFITS OF THIS KIND OF PLATFORM TO BUSINESSES

Lifetime Customer Relationship – Businesses can maintain a lifetime relationship with their clients through one digital ID. They can then ship any package to them without fear of address inaccuracy. They can also make any offer to them using preferred digital channels. In general, businesses can focus on quality of service, selling the right services to the right demographic and not worrying about maintaining accurate personal information about each individual. Consumers tend to transact more when they don't have to expose a lot of personal information.

Financial Compliance – Every transaction in the world could be represented by a single unique QR code. This QR code could capture data related to the entire transaction including details of the buyer and the recipient, transaction location, merchant or businesses involved, payment provider and financial information, various taxes (customs, sales, GST, VAT, etc.), shipper details, location details and delivery instructions. This information is a critical component in managing compliance and cross-border regulations. The QR code could also be used as a shipping label. This offering also prevents leakage of transaction data and shields data between different parties as each party can see only a sliver of the information, based on their role in the transaction.

Identity Verification and Fraud Protection – Every consumer can be verified at multiple layers for demographic and personally identifiable information validation, without the need of collecting and maintaining all the information for every user. Each transaction could automatically capture the audit trail that can be leveraged by different parties based on their roles and the law of the land.

Defaulters Management – It is not uncommon that defaulters, in order to hide in society, keep changing houses and trying to change identity to avoid payback of certain loans. This system would be able to track a consumer leveraging several different digital and physical channels. As the onus is on the recipient to manage their delivery addresses, any changes made for delivery addresses can be tracked.

Cross-Border E-commerce – Some key challenges include accepting various address formats and validating their accuracy during checkout. Today, a small fraction of e-commerce stores in the world allow cross-border transactions. The new EU VAT regulation and US Stop Act governance mandate GDPRS compliance and filing of transaction details to all regulatory authorities such as taxes, customs, banks and so forth. The universal login could enable cross-border capability for any e-commerce store very quickly. The QR code could help to ensure compliance with the financial regulations related to all the parties involved.

Direct Mailing and Marketing – Every business is trying to find prospective consumers for its products and services. The current approach of marketing campaigns, especially when trying to sell everything to everyone, can be a waste of resources. The latest figures from the Direct Marketing Association (DMA) suggest a conversion rate of around 5% for direct mailing or marketing. To improve personalised offers, brands typically collect a lot of personal data such as name, age, gender, purchase history and contact number. A lot of this information can be spoofed, spied and bought from third parties. This makes consumers extremely wary of engaging with such businesses. Several regulatory entities are clamping down on such practices and large brands have been penalised billions of dollars under GDPRS violations. The movie *The Social Dilemma* has exposed how some large companies are collecting and abusing consumer data. This platform gives total control to consumers to decide what demographic information can be shared without sharing personally identifiable information (PII). Consumers can opt in to what they want, when and where they want it, as frequently as they like, without sharing any PII. Essentially, consumers can manage their privacy, whilst brands and businesses can get informed decisions based on validated demographic information.

BENEFITS FOR POSTAL OPERATORS AND LOGISTIC COMPANIES

The use of this kind of platform could empower national operators to become the 'single source of truth' within their country. The QR codes enable automated operations like sorting, routing, tracking and communicating with the customer using omnichannel. Post offices can provide additional services to their consumers. And rather than offer generic hold and pick-up or forward options for packages, efficiencies such as flexible delivery rules at transaction level can be introduced.

Postal operators could then also access and create newer streams of revenue like address and identity verification for digital transactions and physical shipments, and drive opt-in-based direct mailing and marketing. With these opportunities to transform the postal arena, postal operators would be able to expand critical resources to other high-yield channels dedicated to developing and galvanising key strategic relationships with brands, manufacturers, governments, e-commerce players and other third-party shippers (such as FedEx, UPS, Amazon and DHL).

CONCLUSION

The world isn't just changing, it has already changed significantly and will continue to evolve. Postal operators can lead the next generation of transformation by adopting integrated digital solutions. The UPU could lead this transformation by integrating global post offices under a common digital platform, enabling and empowering post offices to transform their digital revolution.

QUESTIONS FOR THOUGHT AND DISCUSSION

1. *There are many digital addressing solutions, as well as many 'legacy' physical addressing protocols. What are the main challenges to overcome in order to achieve the wider adoption of a new concept?*

2. *What are the advantages and disadvantages of having a so-called 'lifetime address'?*

E-COMMERCE LOGISTICS ECOSYSTEMS IN A DIGITAL WORLD

"The bottom line is that data analytics can help improve throughput, reduce operational risk and lower the cost per parcel."

NUMBERS GAME – THE DIGITAL IMPERATIVE

Anders Lildballe

BEUMER Group

INTRODUCTION

Over the past decade, the retail and B2B markets have experienced tremendous growth in e-commerce. Globally, it would be hard to find a CEP company that has not seen an increase in the number of parcels it handles.

This growth represents a massive opportunity for the CEP industry, but it also comes with challenges. In particular, distribution centres have to make adjustments to enable them to keep up with demand and thrive in this new era of soaring e-commerce.

CHALLENGES IN TODAY'S CEP INDUSTRY

PEAK SEASONS

As well as the traditional Christmas shopping period, there now seems to be an almost endless variety of peak shopping seasons – Black Friday, Cyber Monday, Singles' Day, Amazon Prime Day and others. These are great for business but require distribution centres to strike a balance between being prepared for high demand and having massive overcapacity between peaks.

INCREASED COMPETITION

Next-day and even same-day delivery are becoming the norm as webshops and CEP companies compete to provide the best service for their customers. To achieve this standard, distribution centres need to operate more efficiently with fewer hold-ups than ever before.

PARCEL MIX

There is now far greater variety in the sizes and shapes of parcels, with items that have machine-readable labels mixed in with those that demand manual handling, all compounded by different types and standards of packaging. All this contributes to increased complexity in the parcel mix, which requires a more demanding sortation process.

These are just three of the challenges distribution centres currently face, the common thread being that they need to operate extremely efficiently. One of the best and most cost-effective ways for CEP companies to keep up with these demands is through digitalisation, enabling them to operate with efficiency and accuracy in an increasingly complicated industry.

WHAT WILL IT TAKE FOR THE CEP INDUSTRY TO OPEN UP TO DIGITALISATION?

Digitalisation is first and foremost a strategic choice. Many organisations tend to fall in love with technology, followed by the need to find out where it can be applied. This approach will often meet cultural barriers and an internal struggle to communicate the 'why'.

It would be much better to reverse the process and begin with the 'why'. Why is it important for your organisation and what is your digital ambition? To find the answer, it can be helpful to look at how digitalisation can not only help but also change the way an organisation works. How can the change affect the operation in a positive way? With this knowledge, the selection and implementation of the right technology become much easier.

To begin a digital strategy, consider applying two dimensions: (1) the digital ambition – how digital should the organisation become? – and (2) the level of integration – which roles should become digital in the organisation?

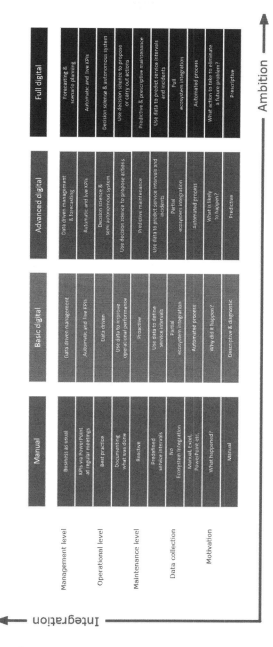

Figure 1[1]

1   https://knowledge.beumergroup.com/hubfs/Data maturity.png

FROM A MANUAL TO A DIGITAL ORGANISATION – THE POTENTIAL OF DIGITALISATION

As a starting point, look at the different levels of digitalisation to determine where your distribution centre is right now. Most CEP organisations will rank in one of the four levels described below. Those at levels 1 and 2 have vast potential to improve their operations through digitalisation.

1. MANUAL OPERATIONS

In the basic pen-and-paper method, the sortation system is typically serviced according to a date on a calendar. Every item of information is written down and stored manually. Breakdowns are handled once they occur. Repairs or optimisations generally take place when they are obviously required or when throughput drops noticeably.

2. BASIC DIGITALISATION

Sensors in automated machinery detect information from the entire sortation system. Information is stored digitally and every part of the system is constantly monitored. Data is collected and provides a clear view of how the system performs. Data serves as an aid to understanding what and why something happened. Operators are data-driven in their work and react when digital predetermined conditions are met.

3. ADVANCED DIGITALISATION

Integration of numerous data sources reveals patterns about the performance of the system, performance in specific situations and probable outcomes. The use of algorithms enables the system to be optimised through prediction at operational as well as equipment levels.

4. FULL DIGITALISATION

This is the prescriptive level, where IT will inform you what action to take to eliminate a future problem identified by the system. At the equipment level, this could include knowing which parts to replace and when to do so. At the operational level, it includes knowing what decisions to make to avoid a bottleneck. Depending on the chosen level of autonomy, the system can propose an action, inform about an action that has been taken, or simply carry out the action itself.

Any distribution centre can benefit from any level of digitalisation and in time advance to a higher level. Generally speaking, it should always be remembered that *all levels of data analytics are valuable and distribution centres can't become fully fledged digital operations overnight!*

MOVING YOUR CEP OPERATIONS TO THE NEXT LEVEL

Without necessarily having to change the layout of sortation systems, distribution centres can benefit from data capture, analytics and other digitalisation efforts according to several criteria, including performance analysis, maintenance and reduced manual handling.

One company whose performance we analysed achieved a 20% improvement in productivity and a 30% increase in outbound trailer fill. At the same time, it was able to reduce the number of manual handling accidents dramatically and achieve better engagement with its staff. All this was accomplished despite the site having a relatively small footprint.

In another distribution centre, three errors seemed to recur frequently: round or unstable items ended up between carriers; loose tape or wrapping got stuck in inductions; and wrapping caused items to stop in the inlets of chutes. Increasingly frustrated by the same errors repeating, managers at the centre realised that they needed a more comprehensive understanding of the sortation system and these recurring incidents. They decided to employ data analytics and hired a systems provider to oversee the effort. Enormous amounts of data from the sortation system were collected and analysed, and the complete processing journey of each item was mapped out.

As data was analysed, every item told its own tale of how the sortation system was operated and how it responded to certain events. As the number of tales grew, so did the distribution centre's understanding of why the same errors recurred. For example, the centre identified that one webshop had started to wrap products in tape. These were not difficult products to process per se, and identical products from other webshops were handled without difficulty. It was the tape itself that was causing the problem – a discovery that enabled the centre to work out a more desirable wrapping solution with the client.

CONCLUSION

The bottom line is that data analytics can help improve throughput, reduce operational risk and lower the cost per parcel. CEP businesses have felt the considerable impact of the e-commerce tsunami at both the B2B and B2C levels and the COVID-19 pandemic has certainly accelerated this trend. This has further underlined the possibilities and opportunities for digital transformation.

QUESTIONS FOR THOUGHT AND DISCUSSION

1. *With such clear benefits from digital automation of parcel sorting, why are many still operating with manual or basic digital operations? What are the barriers to digital ambition?*

2. *How can investment and project time-cycles keep up with the pace of technological innovation?*

"the challenge for efficient supply-chain management is to use all this data to improve service at all levels: transport time, prediction and cost, volume balancing and location optimising in warehouses."

FULFILMENT CENTRES AND THEIR PIVOTAL ROLE IN LOGISTICS

Jacob Johnsen

lpostes.com

INTRODUCTION

We know Amazon, Alibaba, eBay and others for their e-commerce platforms. But for many of their customers, these are not only places for selling: they also provide large and efficient fulfilment centres. Here, they hold the goods as well as ensure pick, pack and ship to the end customers. But they go far beyond simple warehousing.

These fulfilment centres are not only used by their owners but also by other companies, be it manufacturers or traders. Other companies will either ship themselves or leave this task to a broad variety of fulfilment centres that have enhanced and specialised the discipline of acting as the shippers' logistic partner. When acting between marketplace companies and their end customers, fulfilment centres must be trusted by the sender to represent them, and to provide both sender and recipient with the physical and the digital interface between them.

This chapter will explain why fulfilment centres are playing an increasing role in the full logistic delivery chain, and how their role is closely tied to the business strategy of their customers. What are the challenges and opportunities for fulfilment centres, and how will they have to change and adapt to stay relevant? And what is the ultimate goal?

THE DEVELOPMENT OF THE LOGISTIC CHAIN

It all starts with producers having goods that must reach their customers. In this simple form, the producer holds a stock of goods and sends his lorry out to deliver these to his customers. This is often called first-party logistics, or 1PL for short. But quickly a transporter or carrier steps in and ensures the delivery, releasing the producer from having their own lorries, drivers and so forth. The transporter is a second-party logistics provider, thus 2PL.

Today there are a massive number of 3PLs, third-party logistics providers, that will pick up goods from the producer, hold them in store, then ensure delivery to customers as orders come in. Many transporting companies offer a warehousing service, and many warehouses also offer transportation. Yet this is still a relatively limited part of the delivery chain, and the producer is still responsible for requiring pick-up of produced goods and of transferring received orders to the fulfilment centre.

So, 3PL is often not enough.

Currently, there is a steep increase in demand for integrated logistics, and many fulfilment centres are struggling to keep up. Companies not only want the optimum service for their delivery chain, but they also require visibility throughout the chain for both the flow of goods and the applied logistic strategic approach. Many are willing to outsource all logistic processes, but still want to ensure that logistic choices are adapted to their specific business requirements and their delivery strategy.

THE RISE OF 4PL, 5PL AND BEYOND

When having trucks and a warehouse with pick and pack is no longer enough, some fulfilment centres will expand their reach. The fulfilment centres will oversee the entire logistical flow, and select the operator best suited for transporting, warehousing, kitting, packing and distribution. Sometimes this fourth-party logistic operator (4PL) does not own any of the fulfilment centres (then called a 5PL), but usually this will be a natural expansion of an existing setup.

Customers are looking for complete supply-chain solutions, so there is an increased interest in 4PLs and 5PLs. With this, a one-stop shop is effectively provided for all the logistics needs of a customer. The natural next step is to do this for multiple customers, and while adapting each supply chain to the customers' needs and logistic strategy, the wider possibilities for bundling, aggregating and optimising the general logistic capability can be exploited.

FULFILMENT CENTRES GOING DIGITAL

The foundation here is digitisation. While the challenge for single logistic operators is in knowing and predicting volumes, keeping track of every movement, and reporting events, the challenge for efficient supply-chain management is to use all this data to improve service at all levels: transport time, prediction and cost, volume balancing and location optimising in warehouses. The discipline here is the use and application of big data.

With the right data from each step of the process, it is possible to optimise everything from pick-up of goods, transport and delivery to warehouse and placement within warehouse locations – plus all the same steps for goods going out from the warehouse. This is being done today by some advanced fulfilment centres. On top of this, many warehouses use algorithms to optimise exactly where to place goods, based on how often goods are moved in or out, so that slow movers are placed on the top shelves and fast movers are within easy reach.

If planned carefully, the fulfilment centre will have a long string of data associated with every item going into and leaving the warehouse, such as where it originated, all that happened to it and where it was delivered to. Based on many millions or billions of items, such data can be examined. Big data is an important discipline to understand when optimising a complete supply-chain solution. Patterns can be used to find weak spots in the flow and to evaluate each subfunction carefully. The outcome can be used to offer new complete supply-chain solutions and to find areas where customers can be grouped for specific improvements.

FURTHER ADVANCES

Already now, several providers aim to offer producers greater transparency even if transport and warehousing are provided by other companies. This type of partnership, where an array of transporter and fulfilment centres work together, opens up the possibility for more advanced use of the collected data and can give companies the best mix for their supply chain, where the mix of transport and warehousing is optimal – within the selection available to the logistic network provider.

There are further advances in optimising fulfilment centres, either as standalone operations or as part of a network of centres. Some refer to 6PL as the level where the use of AI (artificial intelligence) is used to monitor and optimise a fully integrated and partly automated supply chain. Although not implemented yet on a wider scale, the potential for use of AI in this way is remarkable: monitoring of each step could reveal trends and this could be used to adapt the entire logistic chain or to report anomalies.

Efficiency will often lead to improved sustainability, as simplicity and speed normally lead to reduced use of resources. However, there can be some occasions where the optimum choice for efficiency or service conflicts with the requirements of sustainability and a green approach. This must be factored into all decision making.

The ultimate goal is a delivery system that is self-aware and runs itself through AI and data mining. Although this may seem far-fetched, it is nonetheless part of the high-level strategy of several of the most advanced supply-chain providers. Amazon openly states that one day it may ship items to customers before they actually order them, and Cainiao Logistics, part of Alibaba Group, has similar ideas of being ahead of demands.

CONCLUSION

It is in the interests of both producers and customers that fulfilment centres are fast, efficient and low cost. This can be managed with increased digitisation of all processes and intensive use of data mining and AI. However, ahead of introducing such changes, fulfilment centres must define to what level they will provide a part of the logistic supply chain, be it 3PL, 4PL or beyond.

To provide a full and complete logistic supply-chain offer, the fulfilment centres of the future must either have the ability to monitor every movement of goods and exploit the data from this to optimise, group and consolidate the entire chain, or partner with others that can help to complete the task. This can enable 6PL and beyond.

QUESTIONS FOR THOUGHT AND DISCUSSION

1. *How can postal, transport and logistics operators ensure that they also get benefits from the evolution taking place in fulfilment centres? Does the continuous optimisation in fulfilment centres constitute a threat to the postal, parcel and logistics sector?*

2. *What will customers demand from their future logistic delivery chain? Will it be speed and cost only, or will other factors like clean environment, good working conditions and data security play a role?*

"Why do consumers choose out-of-home delivery and make the active choice to overcome the inertia of the default option to deliver to the home address?"

BUILD IT AND WILL THEY COME?

Tom Forbes and Alex Johnston-Smith

Metapack

INTRODUCTION

Popular wisdom assures us that, if you build a facility, customers will come, but is this true for the infrastructure that supports out-of-home delivery for e-commerce parcels?

There are an estimated 1.4m pick-up/drop-off (PUDO) locations in the world and yet their adoption for parcel collections varies enormously depending on which country they are in. We will use insights from Metapack's original research into tens of millions of out-of-home shipments and the proprietary *Three I Model* to help understand this pattern before making recommendations where out-of-home delivery has yet to achieve scale.

OUT-OF-HOME E-COMMERCE DELIVERIES

When looking at the percentage of e-commerce deliveries that are made out of home, there are marked geographical differences. The Nordic countries and China achieve over 40%; continental European countries like France and Germany are over 20%; by contrast, other significant e-commerce markets like the UK and USA manage less than 1%. Why is this?

At first glance, it looks as if the role of the national post operators could be a cause. Many of the countries with the highest adoption rates of out-of-home delivery are those in which the post has the leading PUDO network. However, the exceptions challenge this narrow explanation.

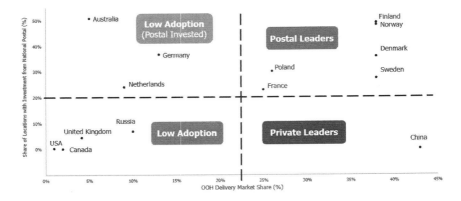

Figure 1[1]

PUDO NETWORKS AND USE OF PUDOS

In fact, most existing studies have tried to answer the question of varied adoption by analysing the PUDO networks themselves. Is this perhaps because the data about the locations has been more readily available? However, the various underused PUDO networks around the world which share the physical characteristics of the successful networks challenge this approach. A viable collection point does not necessarily mean that an individual consumer will make an active choice to direct online orders to it. This paper uses shipment data to test the interaction between consumer choice and the PUDO points themselves to find the reasons why out-of-home delivery has prospered in some countries but not others.

The most helpful framework to separate the different factors is the *Three I Model*:

- *Inertia* – Consumers need a compelling reason to try an out-of-home delivery.

- *Installation* – The PUDO locations need to provide a satisfying experience to motivate the consumer to repeat out-of-home delivery.

- *Integration* – Consumers need the ability to find their desired PUDO option in most of their preferred online retailers' checkouts.

---

1   Source: APEX – Global Parcel Shops & Locker Networks: Market Insight Report 2019 and Metapack observation based on insight from multiple sources

Why do consumers choose out-of-home delivery and make the active choice to overcome the *inertia* of the default option to deliver to the home address? Is it cheaper or is there a high risk of failed delivery to the home?

The research was quick to rule out price as the primary motivation. There was some correlation between the shipping charges offered by retailers and the delivery decisions made by consumers but the national patterns regarding out-of-home delivery prevailed. However, the research did establish a link between the countries with a high percentage of out-of-home delivery and those countries with a high proportion of the population living in apartments.

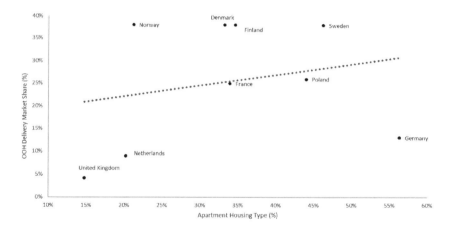

Figure 2[2]

The pattern is even clearer when cross-referenced with data about city living, household ownership and/or local crime. Renters of apartments in higher-crime urban areas are the most likely to choose out-of-home delivery.

How much does the *installation* matter? The research debunked several myths and revealed the following: dense national networks contain numerous under-utilised locations and specialists have been very successful with a few high-quality locations; 'divert in flight' to a PUDO location via SMS or app is disliked by consumers, as evidenced by the long times the parcels wait prior to collection at the PUDOs; and there is little evidence to show that consumers choose to collect parcels as part of their regular journeys to and from home.

---

2   Source: housing type data from Europa.eu; market share data is a Metapack observation based on insight from multiple sources

Instead, the data points to two clear features which lead to an individual location becoming very well used. Firstly, branding matters. PUDOs co-located with nationally recognised retail chains consistently outperform the greater numbers of those located within independent traders. In the UK, 19% of consumers chose a branded location over a closer independent. Secondly, PUDO is a 'winner takes all' market. The data shows that each PUDO has a potential catchment radius of up to 3km at most, and where PUDOs from different networks have overlapping catchment areas, the consumers disproportionately favour one PUDO above all others, irrespective of which network it belongs to.

Lastly, the research looked at the effect of *integration*. There was clear evidence that the way individual retailers design their online checkouts influences consumer behaviour. Underneath the national patterns, the adoption of out-of-home delivery varies up to tenfold from one retailer to another, based purely on the way shipping options are presented. The evidence clearly shows that the retailers that give the consumer a single specific out-of-home delivery option displayed alongside home delivery in the checkout have the highest rates of adoption. Only limited numbers of consumers are prepared to click through various tabs and menus to find the one best suited to their needs.

INSIGHTS FROM THE RESEARCH

Overall, the insights are clear. Out-of-home delivery is particularly relevant to those who share access to their front door and do not want to rely on their neighbours; they have a compelling reason to overcome the *inertia* of the default delivery option. The leading PUDO operators are those that offer quality rather than quantity, and thus the best individual *installations*. A ready market and a good service are all for naught if out-of-home delivery options are not elegantly displayed in most retailers' checkouts. Why then is their *integration* such a challenge?

Most large retailers find *integration* challenging because of the complex mix of technologies supporting their online selling channels. The checkout is usually the preserve of the gurus of basket conversion and platform availability. Integrating and displaying many PUDO locations in the checkout rarely becomes one of a retailer's top priorities.

Additionally, the financial incentive for the largest retailers is not clear. The largest retailers and their carriers invest significant resources in negotiating the final penny of the national home-delivery rate. However, out-of-home delivery offers carriers a clear means of reducing cost every time they deliver a second and subsequent consignment to a PUDO location rather than the procession of home deliveries. Too often this potential saving is not shared with the retailer, because the PUDO model is not mature and the savings cannot be realised without scale. Without the financial incentive of a saving, the retailer is left facing an additional cost to integrate the PUDO locations into their checkouts.

CONCLUSION

In conclusion, our recommendations for PUDO operators, posts and carriers are to:

> *Identify* the software partners of the largest retailers and work with them to ensure all PUDO options are easily displayed in the checkout
>
> *Identify* the software providers that specialise in generic shopping baskets for smaller retailers and work with them to ensure that all PUDO options are easily displayed in the checkout
>
> *Develop easy-to-install APIs* for everyone else
>
> *Lower the price* of out-of-home deliveries to the largest retailers in anticipation of the savings which will follow at higher adoption rates
>
> *Focus on improving the quality* of the individual PUDO locations, especially in areas which contain a high number of apartments, renters, students and higher rates of crime.

Our recommendations for retailers are to:

> *Make retail stores available as PUDO points* in partnership with carriers, even for retail competitors' parcels
>
> *Identify software providers* that make it easy to work with multiple PUDO operators and carriers to ensure that all the leading PUDOs in a market are convenient for consumers
>
> *Present a single out-of-home delivery option* alongside home delivery in the checkout.

QUESTIONS FOR THOUGHT AND DISCUSSION

1. *What are the benefits for operators and retailers from presenting end consumers with a single out-of-home delivery option as an alternative to home delivery? Could this be a critical factor for the continued growth and development of e-commerce?*

2. *What is the scope for collaboration between operators to consolidate PUDO locations in urban areas? What could be the advantages of this and why might it be difficult to achieve?*

SECTION 3
EXPLORING NEW FRONTIERS OF BUSINESS SUSTAINABILITY

MORE SUSTAINABLE BUSINESS

"There is still a gap between consumers' high level of interest in greener postal products and what the market can currently offer profitably."

GREEN POSTAL PRODUCTS – CAN THEY BENEFIT POSTAL OPERATORS AND CONSUMERS?

Jean-Philippe Ducasse

USPS Office of Inspector General[1]

INTRODUCTION

For posts and other delivery companies, environmental sustainability is no longer only about meeting a long-term goal to reduce carbon emissions and contribute to the United Nations' Sustainable Development Goals (SDGs). In recent years, it has also become a product marketing issue – in fact, 56% of US customers have reported being 'very' or 'slightly' concerned about the environmental impact of the delivery of their package.[2] To respond to such consumers' concerns, shippers' requests and city governments' interest in greener deliveries, posts have started to embed environmentally friendly features in their products. This chapter, which builds on a white paper issued by the USPS Office of Inspector General (USPS OIG) in 2020, discusses different types of green postal products from a customer and business perspective.[3]

---

1   The views expressed herein are solely those of the author and do not necessarily reflect those of the US Postal Service Office of Inspector General.

2   Source: USPS OIG survey. In the UK, likewise, 57% of online shoppers worry that the rise in online shopping is a threat to the environment (Parcel and Postal Technology International, 2 December 2020, https://www.parcelandpostaltechnologyinternational.com/news/delivery/uk-consumers-unwilling-to-pay-for-green-shipping-initiatives.html).

3   US Postal Service Office of Inspector General, Sustainability and the Postal Service: Creating a Greener Future Through Product Innovation, Report Number RISC-WP-20-005, 5 August 2020, https://www.uspsoig.gov/sites/default/files/document-library-files/2020/RISC-WP-20-005.pdf

CARBON OFFSETS

To help ensure carbon neutrality, posts can give their customers – mailers and shippers or recipients – the choice of paying more for the carbon compensation of their letter or parcel deliveries. In practice, the post buys carbon-offset credits from a partner, often a carbon-offset non-profit. In a common version of the concept, the partner organisation uses the funds it receives from the post to implement actual carbon-reducing projects – for example, reforestation projects.

The USPS OIG studied 18 posts and logistics companies and found that 13 of them had put in place carbon compensation programs. In some cases (for example, La Poste, Austria Post and Finland Post) they offer free carbon compensation on some or all of their letters or parcels products. Others (such as PostNL and UPS) offer it as a paying option. While USPS does not offer compensation, 53% of US consumers stated they would be willing to pay – on average $0.32 per package – to support carbon offsetting efforts.[4]

Unfortunately, there is no clear evidence that carbon compensation programs in the logistics industry are successful. Customers' appetite for free shipping may take precedence over their willingness to pay for decarbonised deliveries. Besides, these options are not widely advertised, nor are they necessarily available to customers in online shopping carts.[5] Finally, the effectiveness of carbon compensation programs has been questioned. To respond to this last criticism, Deutsche Post DHL is promoting 'carbon insetting'. In this model, offset funding is directed to address impacts inside the logistics supply chain – in other words, it may help pay for the post's own electrical vehicles, not for tree planting in Africa.[6] One advantage of carbon insetting, the authors argue, is that its benefits – such as local improved air quality – are easier to communicate to consumers.

SUSTAINABLE MAILING AND PACKAGING MATERIALS

In the mid-2000s, posts started implementing what probably was one of the earliest forms of environmentally friendly features: the use of sustainable shipping

---

4   USPS OIG survey
5   For example, in Switzerland, 3% of e-commerce merchants offer compensation as an option (Swiss Post, Online retailer survey 2020: Sustainability in Swiss e-commerce, 2020, https://e-commerce.post.ch/onlinehandel-2020/pdfs/EN/Online_retailer_2020.pdf).
6   Deutsche Post DHL and Smart Freight Centre, Carbon Insets for the Logistics Sector, White Paper, November 2020, https://www.dpdhl.com/content/dam/dpdhl/en/media-center/media-relations/documents/2020/dgf-carbon-insets-white-paper-smart-freight.pdf

materials. For many years, the US Postal Service's Priority Mail boxes – one of the free shipping supplies available in post offices – have been meeting Sustainable Forestry Initiative˚ or Forest Stewardship Council˚ certification standards. This means that the paper for the boxes comes from well-managed forests. Boxes also include at least 30% recycled content and are 100% recyclable.

Sustainable advertising mail goes one step beyond, in that it encourages mailers to follow best environmental practices. The post grants a specific green discount to marketing mailers that meet strict sustainability requirements and standards for the sourcing of paper and ink, and for the production and recyclability of their mailings. Royal Mail (Sustainable Advertising Mail), CTT Portugal Post (DM Eco) and PostNord have used this model for more than ten years. The Portuguese Post has said that this product represented about 25% of its total direct-mail volume.

The US Postal Service's Secure Destruction service is another variant of this model. It allows large mailers to opt in to have their undeliverable-as-addressed (UAA) mail returned to USPS facilities for secure destruction, as opposed to being transported and returned to them. USPS promotes the service as an opportunity to improve environmental performance: destroying 25,000 pieces of undeliverable mail – instead of returning it all the way to the sender – saves one metric ton of CO_2.

COLLECTING CONSUMER WASTE

In this model, sustainability is no longer a product feature – it is the main value proposition: the post collects waste and hands it over to recycling companies. Nestlé's Nespresso has partnerships with posts to allow customers to drop off used coffee pods at local postal partner shops (Groupe La Poste) or in mailboxes for carrier pick-up (Swiss Post's Recycling at Home). SingPost (ReCYCLE program) and USPS (Blue Earth Federal Recycling Program) collect used small electronic waste. Groupe La Poste's Recygo subsidiary collects office paper waste and used electronics from businesses throughout France.

PACKAGING AS A SERVICE: REUSABLE PACKAGING SOLUTIONS

In the US, nearly one-third of solid waste comes from packaging, and most of it from e-commerce shipments. At first glance, reusable packaging solutions seem to be an obvious answer to the need to eliminate unnecessary packaging. An overwhelming majority (76%) of US consumers support this idea. Furthermore, about two-thirds said they would be more inclined to choose USPS if it offered this service.[7]

To some extent, reusable packaging is an updated version of the milkman, who would go house to house picking up old milk bottles while delivering new ones. It embodies what the circular economy is about: the customer returns empty packaging to a third-party company that cleans it up, sanitises and reconditions it, then ships it back to e-merchants for a new shipping and return cycle. A number of start-ups offer the service in Europe or the US. Some use recycled polypropylene or vinyl mailers designed for the shipping of lightweight items such as clothing (RePack, Limeloop) or jewellery (Packoorang). Loop, Liviri and LivingPackets, to name a few, have developed sturdy boxes for use for the delivery of heavier merchandise, such as groceries or wine. They sell the packaging to e-commerce merchants and charge them a fee for the return and reconditioning phases.[8]

So far, posts and logistics companies' views on reusable packaging are mixed. Several operators (including Swiss Post, Groupe La Poste and UPS) are testing its operational feasibility and exploring opportunities for co-branding. Strategic uncertainties abound. Unless they are incentivised to do so, will customers return empty packaging? Will e-merchants absorb the extra cost of the service or will they try to pass it on to online buyers? Finally, the COVID-19 crisis has heightened concerns about sanitisation. Overall, in the absence of low-cost solutions, there does not (yet) seem to be a clear, profitable business model for reusable packaging.

GREENER, SLOWER, CHEAPER LETTERS AND PACKAGES

Relaxed performance standards can give a postal operator more flexibility to choose cheaper and potentially more environmentally friendly ways of handling letters – for example, by eliminating air transportation. La Poste's Green Letter (a two-day product) generates 30% less CO_2 emissions than the one-day Priority Letter. In Sweden, moving the single-piece letter standard from one to two days allowed the post to cut both costs and CO_2 emissions. In the US, 72% of customers said they would be willing to use such a slower, greener letter product. In fact, half of them would accept at least two more delivery days if it was 10% cheaper than a regular (First Class Mail) letter.[9]

---

7   USPS OIG survey
8   Empty packages are mailed back (creating a new stream for the post), picked up by the carrier or left with a local partner shop or post office.
9   USPS OIG survey

A GREENER LAST MILE

Green delivery through sustainable means is not yet – or only marginally – a product feature. At the end of 2020, less than 1% of UK online shopping outlets offered a carbon-neutral delivery option. At the same time, delivery companies are implementing major initiatives to 'decarbonise' deliveries, ranging from investments in electric vehicles to the piloting of new urban logistics models. The latter often involve the setting up of micro-hubs in city centres, delivery by cargo bikes and sometimes (as in the case of bpost's Ecozone project) a dense network of parcel lockers. Many initiatives are conducted in close collaboration with city governments, in support of their plans to fight congestion and pollution in downtown areas. The numerous examples include DHL in New York City and Miami, Royal Mail with the Aberdeen City Council and Groupe La Poste with the City of Paris.

It remains to be seen whether these environmentally friendly last-mile processes will translate into new products or product features. This may happen whenever delivery companies' and cities' goals align with citizens' expectations. An example of this is off-hours deliveries: 64% of urban Americans said they would welcome more frequent delivery of their packages in the evening, which reduces congestion, CO_2 emissions and delivery costs.[10] This may open the door to a wider range of customised delivery time windows. Another environmentally friendly, albeit controversial, concept is to consolidate all last-mile deliveries for a given area, restricting them to a single delivery company. This theoretical last-mile public utility model could, for example, result from a local government's decision to give this company a monopoly over all parcel deliveries within that area. When prompted about the concept, 39% of Americans indicated that they liked it, but 29% stated that they disliked it.[11] Widespread worries about undue regulation, possible price increases or reduced service quality may balance customers' positive expectations of environmental and efficiency benefits.

CONCLUSION

There is still a gap between consumers' high levels of interest in greener postal products and what the market can currently offer profitably. In fact, aside from notable exceptions like recyclable packaging, the green product specifications

---

10   USPS OIG survey. In New York City, off-hours deliveries generate 26% less greenhouse gas emissions than regular deliveries.

11   USPS OIG survey

discussed above are emerging or marginal innovations. In the coming years, increased pressure from shippers, consumers and governments should speed up the transition to more scalable business models. In this respect, reusable packaging and green urban delivery both have the potential to become mainstream features.

In addition, we can expect environmental friendliness to become a key feature of all postal products, *whether or not marketed as 'green'*. Postal marketers worldwide will need to treat the environmental impacts of all letter or package products on a par with other specifications such as price and delivery standards. They will also have to include them in all their business plans and marketing strategies.

QUESTIONS FOR THOUGHT AND DISCUSSION

1. *What are the main reasons why green postal products and services have not yet taken off and become mainstream?*

2. *It could be argued that businesses should aim to ensure that every single activity of their business becomes fully sustainable in every sense of the word, and not just their products and services. Discuss.*

"To achieve those cost savings and reduce their sensitivity to volume peaks, posts need to be able to increase consolidation and move more parcels in less time."

HOW TO STOP THE USO FROM BECOMING AN ACHILLES' HEEL

Mike Richmond and Ethan Morgan

Doddle

INTRODUCTION

Universal service obligations are a powerful differentiator for posts. They provide a sense of history, built on customs from a previous era but remaining relevant and working to ensure collection, delivery and counter services are available to everyone and anyone. These traditions and practices, especially universal service, remain fundamental to the identity of posts around the world today.

During the COVID-19 pandemic, we have seen several initiatives by posts that exemplify this, reinforcing their position as universal service providers of essential services. AnPost launched a brilliant 'Send Love' free postcard scheme which highlighted their ability to connect all communities including remote and vulnerable citizens. Another example was La Poste's *'veillez sur mes parents'* service, where the postie 'checked-in' on elderly relatives for a small fee. These are just two examples of posts positioning their brands on service and community, whilst also majoring on their universal service obligation as a means of differentiating their brand to compete in an increasingly competitive parcel delivery market.

However, universal service obligations also present some fundamental challenges. They can make posts vulnerable to disruption in two important ways: firstly, from competition picking off their most profitable routes and leaving the low-density, margin-erosive routes for the post; and secondly, from volume peaks where other parcel carriers can more easily navigate demand by choosing who to serve and how much to charge.

HOW THE USO LEADS TO SERVICE DISRUPTION

A clear example of this is currently playing out in the US parcel market. UPS and FedEx are the dominant private carriers (for the time being, at least – Amazon is aggressively growing its own last-mile delivery operation). During the winter holiday season in 2020, both UPS and FedEx introduced unprecedented surcharges on residential B2C deliveries, creating higher prices to compensate for the increased cost per parcel of those domestic deliveries compared with the B2B deliveries they have built their businesses upon. In doing so, UPS and FedEx effectively used market economics to create a segment of higher-margin customers and deliveries which they retained for themselves, and priced the rest out, in what one well-respected analyst referred to as "hiring and firing their customers".

And the consequence of this behaviour by UPS and FedEx is that someone else must pick up the less-profitable volume that UPS and FedEx do not want – and in the US that falls to the United States Postal Service. The national postal operator is left to manage UPS and FedEx's cast-off customers during the biggest peak surge in history, which was inevitably a huge challenge, even before accounting for COVID-19 workplace restrictions and unwell employees, which reduced the post's capacity.

USPS delivers a huge volume of parcels every year and does so incredibly effectively, but the fact remains that its quasi-public status, the USO and regulatory constraints prevent it from doing the same thing as FedEx and UPS, and so, as a post, it must find a way to deliver those less-profitable parcels. The question then becomes whether or not a post can prevent the demands of the USO and competitors' 'cherry-picking' behaviour from resulting in long-term decline of market share. We believe the answer is yes, they can.

POSTS CANNOT USE THE STICK, BUT THEY CAN USE THE CARROT

In general, because of the impact of other carriers cherry-picking profitable volume, posts must be very focused on capacity management and flexibility, because they do not have as much control over their incoming volume of parcels. However, it is simply not economical for them to have the necessary infrastructure and resource capacity for peak delivery all year round when such infrastructure and capacity would lie fallow for much of the year. Without such additional resources, then, the best alternative is for posts to find ways to maximise the effectiveness of their existing resources.

Posts have one crucial advantage over their competition in this space: their extensive real estate. Having a network of well-established post offices gives posts crucial geographic coverage and reach for their PUDO efforts, in a way that carriers struggle to match without years and years of investment and building. The Post Office in the UK, for example, has *c.* 11,000 locations and is at the heart of every community. Harnessing that infrastructure and pricing its utilisation appropriately could lead to huge cost savings for posts that are particularly sensitive to peaks in parcel volumes.

To achieve those cost savings and reduce their sensitivity to volume peaks, posts need to be able to increase consolidation and move more parcels in less time. To incentivise more consolidation, posts can start to use pricing as a positive motivator. In effect, this could look like the opposite of the FedEx–UPS strategy, where pricing increases for 'bad' or 'difficult' deliveries, as in this case posts would instead offer a discount for a consolidated, out-of-home delivery.

Such pricing already exists in several markets – France, Poland and Sweden all price pick-up services at a 20–25% discount to home delivery. And many commentators see the market moving towards out-of-home delivery: *"Five to seven years from now, my feeling is that door-to-door deliveries are going to be 40 percent of the market or less"* (Rafal Brzoska, founder and CEO, InPost).

If such forecasts are even remotely accurate, posts are in a strong position to capitalise, thanks to their infrastructure advantages and extensive networks.

A SPLIT DELIVERY MODEL FOR THE FUTURE, BALANCING OUT-OF-HOME AND HOME DELIVERY

Consolidating parcels is always good for margins and capacity, but it is especially effective when the alternative is going door to door in particularly sparsely populated areas – just the type of route that carriers would prefer not to serve at the same price as a city. If a post can entice shoppers to pick up parcels from single locations like grocery stores, which are already frequented by consumers, the delivery cost saving is potentially huge compared to driving to each individual door. Passing some of that saving on to retailers allows them to offer consumers even cheaper delivery when they select a consolidated option, like pick-up at a PUDO location. That is the incentivisation and pricing lever that is available to posts.

CONCLUSION

Whereas private carriers can easily say up-front to a retailer that the price has increased for certain postcodes, posts need to use the incentive of cheaper rates for volumes which can then be consolidated, so that they can stay competitive and become more cost-effective and less vulnerable to volume peaks.

QUESTIONS FOR THOUGHT AND DISCUSSION

1. *Accepting all items presented and maintaining the USO with costly deliveries to rural and remote areas whilst, at the same time, trying to be a profitable commercial business is a huge challenge faced by many postal operators. Can the ideas set out here help to solve this challenge and, if so, what do they need to do to implement this strategy, and what might be some of the implications?*

2. *What are the advantages and disadvantages of flexing your pricing up or down? Why might you want to do this (e.g. to manage demand, to deal with additional costs)? Is it easier to put up prices or to reduce or discount them?*

"Posts in today's world are increasingly facing challenges they haven't encountered before, for which they don't have all the answers. How can we make a successful digital transformation?"

HOW TO ADAPT TO THE 'VUCA TIMES' – MANAGING UNCERTAINTY

Yu Yan

Asian-Pacific Postal Union

INTRODUCTION

You may have heard about an acronym, **VUCA**, which was first coined by the US Military Academy, West Point. This term describes the battlefield of the new era as having four key characteristics: **volatility**, **uncertainty**, **complexity** and **ambiguity**.

Competing in the business world is analogous to fighting on a battlefield. Indeed, today companies face a VUCA environment. The spread of new technologies has disrupted operating models in most industries, including the postal sector. As global markets, supply chains and financial systems become highly interconnected, small problems can have significant ramifications.

Posts in today's world are increasingly facing challenges they haven't encountered before, for which they don't have all the answers. How can we make a successful digital transformation? How can our outlets attract Generation Z customers? How shall we accomplish the shift from letter carrier to parcel carrier? Under the impact of COVID-19, with increased demand on local parcel services but not enough labour, how can we remain as an important player in the last mile?

WHAT DOES 'UNCERTAINTY' MEAN TO OUR ORGANISATIONS

While many leaders know how to cope with *operational uncertainty* – for example, cost fluctuations, profit and loss, operational optimisations, and some internal changes in the industry that can be sensed directly by enterprises – they are less sensitive to another type of uncertainty which is often more dangerous.

Companies in today's world are increasingly facing *structural uncertainty*, which has a direct impact on business growth, product development and decision making. It is caused by changes in customers' demands, substitute product/service solutions, innovative business models and so forth. These sprout silently and grow up quietly, and as a result, leaders often fail to recognise them as elements that will bring pressure and force changes.

For example, just as the emergence of digital cameras structurally subverted traditional film cameras, some new operators specialising in last-mile services may completely disrupt the postal network in the future. Leaders of postal operators that have made arrangements to increase investment in network resources, service capabilities and personnel for the first and last mile reflect greater management sensitivity; and they are thus more likely to spot the catalysts of disruption and therefore build better organisational preparedness.

THE UNCERTAINTIES WHICH COMPANIES FACE ARE BECOMING MORE COMPLEX AND FAST-MOVING

Ram Charan, the world-renowned business advisor, wrote in his book *The Attacker's Advantage: Turning Uncertainty into Breakthrough Opportunities* that "Uncertainty has always been a challenge to business, but never before has it had the intensity and potential to change industries and destroy companies as it does today."

Changes in the past may have been drastic, but now they are more varied and faster moving. Today, relying on established structures, processes and expertise to deal with VUCA is not enough, as new challenges come along with digitisation and integration and at a faster pace than before. These multi-dimensional challenges make today's uncertainty more difficult to respond to.

Life cycles of companies, products and services can also fluctuate dramatically over time. There will always be some operators who manage to provide customers with an 'always-connected' network, unlimited flexibility supported by advanced technology, yet at a low price. However, the 'opportunity window' makes it quite difficult for product and service providers to remain competitive over a longer term. Everyone must run as fast as they can, just to keep up!

FACING THE CHALLENGE

Facing the challenge of VUCA, what are some common mistakes that leaders make in response?

Lack of Cognitive Skills – It is not the technology that is disruptive; instead, it is their logic. When companies have trouble dealing with disruption, it is frequently because they are still aligned with the old logic. Leadership in VUCA times requires a set of behaviours that help organisations to change and move in new directions. Therefore, to cultivate the ability to anticipate and deal with new threats facing the business is the key point.

Inability to Stand with Employees when Uncertainty happens – We know how to make business numbers work, but we do not know how to build strong relationships that are lasting and valued. Taking the example of the situation we have been facing during the pandemic, one of the biggest challenges was whether postal business could operate normally and take the opportunity to market the post's brand. Do we take the initiative whenever possible? It is all directly related to how we treat postal employees. So, whilst striving to improve the service we provide, it is only when employees feel their voices are heard and their efforts are seen, that they can fully engage themselves and excel in their work.

Hesitating in Making up their Minds – Leaders may hesitate when they do not have enough information to know what actions will work best. This situation often occurs when new ideas come out and nobody knows how to realise them. If one uses the traditional teamwork methods, doing careful deployment, thinking first, proceeding step by step, following a pre-designed plan and not risking making mistakes, then innovation may never happen.

TACTICS

What tactics can leaders use to better manage in a VUCA environment?

Enhance Cognitive Thinking – This will allow them to be able to adapt and learn more quickly how to sort out complex problems. Leaders must be able to plan ahead, anticipating major changes whilst also remaining competitive in the present. In a highly uncertain environment, conventional thinking and approaches can fall short. Success in this uncertain context requires new ways to lead. The process of learning, progressing and changing helps leaders to notice trends and build up a new logical understanding of how to get to where they need to be. Leaders may also have to frequently remind employees about uncertainty, interdependence and vulnerability to help them perform well.

Guide the Team with Organisational Values to Make the Right Decisions – The Starbucks value statement is a very good example of this: "We're not in the coffee business serving people, we're in the people business serving coffee". Coffee is not scarce but caring for people is becoming scarcer. This value has shaped Starbucks' brand image as the Third Space in the City. Values support and convey a company's mission and vision, guide management decisions and maintain a team's cohesion. Values direct and motivate a company's attitudes and actions from the inside. During moments when the market is turbulent and public opinion is tense, adhering to values can create a continuing bond between short-term and long-term interests. This can also help the team re-establish and maintain a sense of purpose and make the right decisions in line with long-term values, especially in a crisis.

Diversity in the Service to Achieve Business Capacities – 'Stick to the core or go for more' has always been a hot topic when discussing business strategy. In the industrial age, such debates are only practical when the division of labour in any industrial chain is relatively clear. However, structural uncertainty has disrupted some old logics, and this division is less clear when we move into the internet or digital age. Today, only companies that can offer immediacy, personalisation and accessibility to their customers will win out in the long run. Postal operators must meet customer expectations by going beyond their existing core services to create new value and improve network efficiency and effectiveness.

Build Organisational Agility to Ensure a Higher Degree of Flexibility at all Times – This approach involves quickly mobilising people to cope with a high degree of uncertainty. Under this fast collaboration mode, different people team up at different times, as determined by the shifting demands of a project. Leaders need to create a way to communicate effectively and make the right information visible to the management chain at the right time. Then, different expertise can be brought in to different scenarios when required, encouraging flexible and dynamic cooperation, conducting small experiments to learn as fast as possible about what works and what does not, and establishing mechanisms to organise and prioritise tasks.

Create Psychological Safety – This is so that team members will be willing to speak up with their ideas and critiques. In uncertain situations, key staff must remain highly engaged so that they can offer suggestions and concerns to help the team avoid risks and collaborate to achieve their goals. Therefore, the more uncertain the work environment, the more important psychological safety is. However, providing psychological safety is not about making team members stay in their comfort zones, but rather about allowing them to enter a learning zone, where standards and motivations are both high. It is also important to actively invite team members to participate and speak up. The way to do this involves demonstrating some humility, asking good questions and creating channels for employees to speak up.

CONCLUSION

Determination is a key trait of successful leaders in VUCA times. Uncertainty can result in people becoming more anxious because they feel that they lack control, feel threatened or feel concerned that they will not be able to cope with whatever lies ahead. So, leaders must not panic when uncertainty appears. Instead, they must go against conventional wisdom and admit they do not have all the answers, so the team can have a psychologically safe, learning-oriented work environment. Being open, seeking opinions and ideas from others, and focusing on what is really needed – greater vision, strategic planning and support – are the marks of a good leader. It is certainly not easy!

QUESTIONS FOR THOUGHT AND DISCUSSION

1. *Leading postal organisations through transformation in 'VUCA times' is very challenging and needs exceptional leaders. Where can we find the leaders that the sector needs? How can they best be prepared for taking on these roles?*

2. *What can we learn here from the author about leading employees through difficult, turbulent and uncertain times?*

"by relying on short-lived products and single-use packaging, we will make our planet uninhabitable faster than we all are willing to admit."

REUSABLE PACKAGING

Alvin Dammann Leer

Packoorang

INTRODUCTION

We have a waste problem. Our use-once-and-dispose lifestyle poses a serious threat to our planet and our very existence. Ever-growing mountains of trash are reaching our landfills, where it keeps leaking into nature in the shape of toxins, nano plastic and carbon. Large masses of plastic are infesting our oceans, threatening marine life and upsetting our ecosystems. And before the toys, consumer goods and packaging even reach this 'afterlife' stage, every item must be sourced, manufactured, packaged and distributed – all carbon-intensive affairs.

And the issue is intensifying: e-commerce is growing rapidly amidst lifestyle shifts that were present before the global pandemic and which have only gathered pace during it. At the same time, the global population is rising and developing populations are increasingly able to copy the unsustainable habits of developed nations. Business Wire recently reported that the plastic packaging market is expected to double in the next ten years. If we keep on this path, by relying on short-lived products and single-use packaging, we will make our planet uninhabitable faster than we all are willing to admit.

REUSABLE PACKAGING

Packoorang was born out of this realisation and frustration with the status quo. Today's e-commerce and food industries are laden with trash, from single-use parcels to plastic polybags, from Styrofoam to packing peanuts and bubble wrap. When half of the world's waste comes from packaging and more than 99.9% of packaging is single-use, circularity and reusable packaging is clearly an area of importance, and one which needs to be supported by all stakeholders and policy makers in the coming years. Current calculations show that reusable packaging, able to withstand 100 or more reuses, can reduce carbon footprint by more than 90% and reduce trash generation by a factor of 10–20. These are significant numbers that cannot be overlooked.

Of course, as with anything new there are obstacles. Circular models are still in their infancy, and to make them work at scale, consumers, manufacturers and distributors need to be onboard with the change in approach. Studies show that circular models can be financially beneficial as well as an attractive proposition from a marketing and customer-loyalty perspective, yet there is work to be done to open stakeholders' eyes to the possibilities and benefits. Education and awareness work will be key here. However, considering the ever-increasing pressures on companies to become carbon neutral, we believe the threat of a 'sustainability debt' – a term I coined to describe the costs that companies incur when they do not invest in their sustainability strategy – will provide plenty of incentive for companies to adopt circular models.

CONCLUSION

Beyond awareness, there are a few other challenges with introducing reusable packaging. These include ensuring compatibility with packing machines, incentivising consumers to adopt and comply with the rules of circular packaging, and keeping distribution and asset management tidy at scale. These are all challenges that can be overcome, however, by leveraging technology and sophisticated strategies. Once circular models have matured within the e-commerce and logistics industries, the opportunity is there for brands to gain a competitive advantage over competitors and position themselves for future-proof operation and growth – in a sustainable way.

QUESTIONS FOR THOUGHT AND DISCUSSION

1. *Adopting reusable packaging as part of a more sustainable circular economy in e-commerce is a compelling idea. How can the concept be realised and how can the challenges be overcome? Who needs to collaborate and on what basis?*

2. *The author introduces the concept of a 'sustainability debt', where companies incur more financial penalties later by failing to invest early enough in vital areas. Could this concept be used to encourage companies to commit to all kinds of sustainability initiatives? If so, how?*

MORE SUSTAINABLE URBAN LOGISTICS

"new business models and processes can make postal and logistics operations more sustainable"

URBAN LOGISTICS – NEW CUSTOMER-CENTRIC MODELS

Bernhard Bukovc

Postal Innovation Platform

INTRODUCTION

The flow of goods in large urban areas has always been a challenge. Over the past two decades, the e-commerce boom and changing customer demands have increased the pressure to implement customer-centric strategies.

Beside the changing market environment, delivery companies are faced with public pressure to help reduce traffic, pollution and waste. Our society is demanding more sustainable and greener ways to provide services, in particular in urban environments. Governments are considering implementing, and in certain locations have already implemented, measures and regulations to curb traffic and pollution.

While customers ask for profound changes, delivery companies strive to be competitive and profitable. What has been a delicate balancing act and possibly even considered contradictory in the past is today a business imperative. The good news is that new business models and processes can make postal and logistics operations more sustainable and, in addition, they can also lead to a better quality of service and higher profitability.

URBAN CHALLENGES

According to a recent World Economic Forum (WEF) report, the number of delivery vehicles in the top 100 cities globally will increase by 36% until 2030, increasing emissions from delivery traffic by 32% and congestion by over 21%.[1]

Therefore, delivery companies face important responsibilities and must address several challenges in urban areas. First, they must tackle congestion and other traffic issues to which they contribute, including noise. Then, there is pollution, a major issue which has a huge impact on the life of people living in cities. And finally, the consumers themselves are adding further layers of challenges with changing expectations, demands and buying behaviours. Solving one of these challenges will not be enough. Postal and other delivery companies will have to find a holistic approach and provide answers for a multitude of today's urban challenges. Fortunately, the solutions are available, and many delivery companies have started to transform into modern urban carriers.

OPTIMISING PROCESSES AND INFRASTRUCTURE

Supply chain and delivery processes are complex. They involve technology, IT, a huge amount of data, automation, as well as a large human workforce with many manual touchpoints. Mastering those processes is key to enabling a high-quality and customer-centric service provision. In a highly competitive market, the operators that prevail will have the most efficient processes, at the lowest costs, and offer their customers the solutions and services which they demand.

Implementing a sound urban logistics approach needs to start with the existing infrastructure and, in most cases, it will be possible to have significant efficiency gains with the optimisation of those processes.

Route optimisation and real-time tracking are key parameters in modern urban logistics processes. Cutting the daily driven mileage will help to cut emissions, save costs and allow a smaller delivery fleet. Real-time visibility over processes or changing customer demands (e.g. delivery location) will help to improve route planning and to adapt to new needs quickly, such as with dynamic re-routing. Route optimisation and full visibility of all supply chain and delivery processes must be part of the overall digital transformation strategy of all delivery companies. The first step of implementing a customer-centric urban logistics solution should thus start with existing infrastructure and processes.

---

1   The Future of the Last-Mile Ecosystem, World Economic Forum 2020

NEW BUSINESS MODELS

To respond to the tremendous impetus for change it will not be enough just to adapt the existing infrastructure, but it will also be necessary to develop new business models. There is a huge opportunity to better respond to customer needs, become eco-friendly and open new revenue streams at the same time.

Overall, we can see one driving trend, localisation, and this got a strong additional push during the COVID-19 pandemic. The localisation trend started well before the pandemic, but during the crisis people and businesses needed solutions for local commerce and local supply.

PUDO networks or locker systems are examples of how delivery companies try to get closer to consumers and thus make it more convenient for them to receive parcels, even though it means that they must go somewhere to pick them up. Some start-ups are trying to fill this gap and offer platforms for crowd-based delivery and collection of parcels from PUDO points.[2]

Ship-from-store is another trend which is getting increasingly important. Stores can be considered as local depots, so why not use them to better serve customers, particularly in urban areas, who want fast delivery solutions, such as same-day or same-hour delivery. With traditional business models, such processes are expensive and most probably not ecologically friendly. Ship-from-store solutions can help to enable fast and green delivery models at the same time, thus creating convenient solutions for consumers. Fast does not necessarily mean unsustainable. It can actually mean the contrary, if the business model is right. Moreover, it offers a business proposition to retailers to optimise their outlets and better reach their customers. To this end, DPD has acquired Stuart, a French start-up providing an on-demand logistics platform which helps to transform stores into urban warehouse networks, thus allowing retail stores new ways to reach their customers and customers to receive their ordered goods the same day.[3] Not surprisingly, Uber has started to enter this market segment of local shipments and delivery services as well.[4]

Waste is another issue all delivery companies are confronted with. Linear processes in packaging produce waste. Although cardboard packaging can be recycled, there

---

2   For example, Mister Postman GmbH, a German start-up, provides a platform for crowd-based delivery and collection of parcels (https://mister-postman.net).

3   https://stuart.com

4   https://www.uber.com/newsroom/moving-more-of-what-matters-with-delivery

are the issues of waste disposal and limits to recycling. Increasing pressure from governments imposing taxes on the use of non-reusable packaging increases costs. For the moment, these costs are almost negligible, but this may change in the future. The circular economy is a business model which can help to avoid waste. The objective is that materials stay in the economy and do not become waste or pollution. Reusable packaging is not only eco-friendly, but it also responds to a customer need and can over time even reduce packaging costs. For traditional delivery processes a new business model would be required which would allow consumers to easily return reusable packages. Swiss Post has decided on a strategy in the field of circular economies and is in the process of implementing a complete solution, based on its current Dispobox reusable system. DHL Supply Chain has piloted a closed-loop packaging solution in North America to reduce single-use corrugate/poly bags by switching to a reusable packaging solution.[5] Swiss Post has also started to develop solutions for same-day deliveries without packaging with notime, a company it acquired to develop services in this specific market.[6]

Sharing of infrastructure will be increasingly important. Examples are depots, urban logistics hubs, parcel lockers and other infrastructure. Space in cities is normally limited. Sharing space would thus overcome some of the challenges that delivery companies face in urban areas. In addition, shared infrastructure can reduce the number of trucks and enable multi-modal delivery strategies. La Poste and its urban logistics business, URBY, are working on a clear strategy involving urban logistics hubs, shared with other market players, which would enable eco-friendly deliveries into cities (EV, cargo bikes).[7]

NEW TECHNOLOGIES

For urban logistics, new technologies can offer viable business models that can help to achieve the aforementioned objectives.

Routing technology and real-time visibility offer outstanding results and are the backbone of any customer-centric strategy. Only when carriers have a clear view of

---

5   Both examples were presented and discussed by Swiss Post and DHL at the PIP Online Executive Forum on 'Enhancing the Value of Parcels and Packaging' on 22 April 2020. See also a DHL report at: https://www.dhl.com/content/dam/dhl/global/core/documents/pdf/glo-core-rethinking-packaging-trend-report.pdf

6   More information at: https://www.notime.ch

7   See more on the website of La Poste's URBY at: https://www.urby.fr/actualites/l-actualite-de-la-logistique/amenagement-zone-logistique-urbaine-toulouse

their processes and planning, and when they know where their delivery trucks are, can customer demands be addressed – for example, through dynamic re-routing. Some technologies even go a step further and enable collaborative routing, thus optimally reacting to any traffic situation in a non-egoistic approach.[8]

Many delivery companies do not yet have systems in place which would enable them to communicate with their customers in a real-time and efficient way. This creates many problems, such as unsuccessful delivery attempts, unsatisfied customers, higher mileage, higher costs and waste of resources. With a combination of the right planning and visibility tools on the one hand and an easy-to-use, automated, consumer-focused communication tool on the other, unsuccessful delivery attempts could be minimised or even disappear. Being able to arrange the delivery time and location, and providing choice, flexibility and predictability are cornerstones of good urban logistics solutions.[9]

Technology is a driver for urban logistics solutions, and EV (electric vehicles) are just one example of how delivery companies can address sustainability demands and customer expectations by adapting their fleet to a zero-CO_2 policy or introducing alternative delivery means. Alternative delivery means which reduce emissions, pollution and traffic jams, such as EV or bikes, can be optimally combined with localised infrastructure as described above, such as shared urban hubs or ship-from-store solutions. Several posts are in the process of changing their fleet to today's requirements and introducing new generations of distribution vehicles on various operational levels. An Post, for example, is the first postal service to eliminate carbon emissions in their capital, Dublin, with an ambitious plan for the whole country.[10] In addition, low-noise EV or bicycle delivery during night times can be a powerful element of an urban logistics strategy and, combined with other elements mentioned above, such as dynamic routing or shared multi-brand lockers, can reduce CO_2 emissions by 30%, congestion by 30% and delivery costs by 25% by 2030, according to the WEF.[11]

---

8   The market leader in this area, Graphmasters, a Swiss–German company, shows impressive results with several logistics and delivery companies and from partnerships with cities and car manufacturers (https://www.graphmasters.net).

9   See for example BookIT.net (https://clickandeasy.com) or Ship2MyID, which enables a new delivery experience based on a digital address (http://www.ship2myid.com).

10 An Post has committed to eliminating 50% of carbon from all postal and delivery operations in Ireland by 2025. See more at: https://www.anpost.com/Media-Centre/News/Dublin-becomes-first-Capital-City-globally-with-ze

11 The Future of the Last-Mile Ecosystem, World Economic Forum 2020

PUBLIC SUPPORT AND REGULATION

Urban areas face many challenges and politicians are looking for solutions to fight congestion, pollution and noise. Delivery companies can play a significant role in helping to solve these issues, as explained above. However, governments and policy makers can also help the delivery industry (freight and parcels) to implement viable and sustainable solutions.

Space in urban areas is limited and (local) governments can support logistics companies by providing space and infrastructure, especially when we think about shared delivery hubs with modular delivery means.

Clear regulation would also be very helpful. Today, when we look at autonomous delivery for example, whether with drones or ground robots, clear rules or requirements are often missing or may differ from one country to another, thus creating more confusion than help. There is certainly room for governments to provide more support and help to drive the development of smart urban logistics solutions.

CONCLUSION

Urban areas face many challenges, and postal and logistics companies can be major players in developing smart solutions. This article could only scratch the surface, and new products or solutions are developed every day.

I believe that the ultimate driver for urban delivery concepts needs to be based on economic considerations and customer convenience. The implementation and roll-out of new solutions and products must follow viable and sustainable business models. Otherwise, the transformation will only happen half-heartedly and will not deliver the desired results.

Implementing sustainable and greener solutions is part of the business model. First, customers demand a reduction of CO_2, waste and other forms of pollution, and second, sustainable business models also trigger higher quality, lower costs and higher profitability.

Today, there is a strong case for transforming current traditional delivery models in urban areas into customer-focused, sustainable business models. With a holistic approach, such business models will make urban logistics greener, increase customer experience and convenience, and will enable cost cutting, new revenue streams and overall higher quality of service. The time is right to implement new customer-centric urban logistics models.

QUESTIONS FOR THOUGHT AND DISCUSSION

1. *Is the intense competition in last-mile delivery in urban areas helping or hindering the implementation of new customer-centric and sustainable urban logistics delivery models? What role could greater inter-business collaboration play?*

2. *Who should drive the changes to smarter urban logistics mentioned here – the end consumer, the delivery operators, merchants and e-tailers, or governments and regulators?*

"Communication and linkages between citizens, government and business are key to a sustainable smart city."

THE POST OFFICE IN THE SMART CITY

John Trimble

Tshwane University of Technology

INTRODUCTION

Urbanisation is on the rise. How can cities increase quality of life and reduce inequality while experiencing exponential growth? The smart city is viewed as a solution to this question. The technologies of the Fourth Industrial Revolution make new ways of urban life possible. New ways of producing and delivering goods and services will create new jobs and enhance living. Some jobs will also be eliminated. Will the newly created jobs outweigh the jobs lost? Will this new balance empower people and communities? Is this course toward an ever-smarter city sustainable? Communication and linkages between citizens, government and business are key to a sustainable smart city. The post office services and infrastructure can play a critical role in the future of the smart city. The post office's (PO) role in the logistics of the smart city and its linkages to government, the private sector and the public are presented as different scenarios. The future of the smart city will be determined by the tenacity of the different stakeholders.

THE SMART CITY

Escalating urbanisation has led to complications and degradation in living conditions in the city. The smart city is seen as the solution to all these problems. It is envisioned that the latest technologies will solve problems of service delivery, transportation, crime, waste disposal and wealth inequality, while providing satisfying jobs, ecological balance and making the city more appealing to visitors.

Information and communications technology (ICT) is central to the technology upgrades needed to develop the smart city. The pervasiveness of internet connectivity and increased speed provides the city with the geographical connectivity to collect information and monitor points of concern instantaneously and on a continuous basis. Low-cost, high-speed monitoring devices and sensors connected to the internet provide the internet of things (IoT). This IoT monitors the state of the city, sending this information to the cloud. Artificial intelligence (AI) techniques, machine learning and computational science are used to digest this massive amount of data in real time. Decisions can be made computationally and conveyed back through the cloud to activate sensors, and inform agencies or citizens of what actions to take.

Cloud computing is a key component of the smart city. Information collected by organisations and individuals is stored in redundant centralised server systems. The major cloud computing companies are providing an increasing range of services to manipulate, characterise and visualise this information. A number of these providers, such as IBM and Google, are directly engaging in designing and implementing smart-city options.

Data mining of the information collected through the IoT, cloud services and dedicated computing applications provides ongoing knowledge about a range of concerns. This knowledge can be accumulated in knowledge management systems and used with decision support applications to aid decision making at a central and individual level. The effective allocation of resources is an important mandate of city planners. Data analytics on information collected can assess resource utilisation and recommend future resource allocation.

E-commerce is pervasive, providing the delivery of goods to businesses and individual consumers. The smart city offers a high-quality experience to the customer, from order placement through product/service delivery and maintenance.

E-governance is important from national to local levels. This is particularly significant at the city level, where most of the citizen's business and socialisation is conducted. The smart city can give the citizen access to city regulations and government procedures from filing taxes to vehicle registration. E-governance can also inform citizens of pending legislation and assess public opinions and positions regarding existing and pending legislation and regulations.

Sustainability of the smart city requires recognition of the city as a closed system and addressing a circular-economy approach across the various supply chains in the city.[1] This closed system consists of smart buildings, smart spaces and smart linkages between buildings and spaces in the city. The design and implementation of a smart city should address smart buildings as smart homes, smart companies and smart institutions. Smart institutions cover a range of buildings: schools, hospitals, airports and post offices. Our focus on post offices and postal services in the smart city is linked to the historical role of the post office as a communication link for citizens and businesses.

THE POST OFFICE

The post office (PO) is most often associated with letter mail delivery. This historical role has resulted in significant infrastructure development, employment, community relationships and experience in logistics. All these postal features are most pronounced in urban areas, particularly the most industrially advanced urban areas, which are the settings best positioned for implementing the smart city. The common practices and experiences of postal units mean best practices in the PO role in smart-city development can easily be shared between cities. The international and regional structures of the PO like the UPU, PAPU and SAPOA could all facilitate this knowledge exchange of intelligent postal services.

Intelligent postal services should address smart buildings, smart networks and smart service delivery. Energy generation and utilisation and water utilisation can be assessed and optimised. This process can easily be replicated for the different post offices across the city. The larger the city, the more significant the optimisation of postal networks and service delivery.

The PO is just one of several institutions exploring the use of blockchain in particular and financial technologies in general to engage in secure transactions. This has implications for the PO as a location for money transfers as well as a broader range of banking functions.

The internet of things (IoT) finds its particular implementation through the Post Office with the internet of postal things (IoPT). It has a history with the tracking of letters and parcels. However, there is the potential for monitoring and adjusting

---

1   J. Trimble and H. Phuluwa, Infusing Circular Economy in African Smart Cities, *Proceedings of the 9th International Conference on Appropriate Technology*, pp. 108–19 (Pretoria: INAT, 2020)

a wider range of activities utilising the vehicles, buildings and other structures associated with the post office. Machine learning can be employed on the massive data and information collected from a comprehensive IoPT. The results could automatically adjust lights, traffic signals, alarms and other internet-connected devices, and make service recommendations to PO customers.

SCENARIOS FOR POSTAL INVOLVEMENT IN THE SMART CITY

The scenarios presented reflect the dominance of the three stakeholder groups in the development of the city: the corporate sector, the government and the public. Table 1 highlights the key features of each scenario.

Table 1. Key Features of Three Scenarios of the Smart City

	Corporate Scenario	**Government Scenario**	**Public Scenario**
Focus	Profit driven	Service delivery	Community control
Approach	Top-down	Top-down	Bottom-up
Technology	High tech, capital intensive, privately funded	Balance of high tech with employment gains, tax funded	Open source, lower costs; crowdsourcing and non-profit funded
Managing technique	Centralised, autocratic through multinational corporations (MNCs)	Centralised, democratic through elected representation	Decentralised, democratic through community control
Supply chain	Private-sector controlled	Government controlled	Citizen controlled
Jobs	Job reduction	Job maintenance	Job creation
Role of post office (PO)	Privatised parcel delivery and many government services, sell off PO assets, reduces PO	Uses PO as logistics and communication link for many government services	PO as site for community training, start-ups and linking open-source projects
Quality of life (QoL)	High QoL for wealthy, low risk for controlling agents	Balanced QoL, low risk	Highest potential to increase QoL, high risk

THE CORPORATE-DRIVEN SMART CITY

Most large multinational (MNC) information-technology-related companies have plans and projects for smart cities. IBM, Siemens, Intel and Google have initiated efforts from Toronto to Rio to provide citywide services to convert urban settings into smart cities. MNCs use their access to technology and capital to drive this model. While they partner with public administrations, their main focus is support for profit-driven private partners in a supply chain that maximises their MNC profit and control. They take a top-down approach focused on increased productivity that generally leads to job reduction. Their privatisation approach leads to a reduced role for state-run postal services. Many of the technology-intensive services that the PO could provide are maintained by the hosting MNC or their junior private-sector partners. The reduced role of the PO in the MNC smart city will lead to further privatisation, loss of postal jobs and dismantling of the PO. The centralised, autocratic management styles of MNCs allow for quick and decisive planning and development of the smart city but provide little room for democratic citizen input.

THE GOVERNMENT-SPONSORED SMART CITY

City managers, city councils and mayors have an interest in delivering a smart city that satisfies their urban constituency. This top-down centralised approach has more accountability to citizens than the MNC smart city. When citizens are empowered, they demand a balanced increase in quality of life, job security and information security in the implementation of the smart city. The government can use the PO as the key logistics and communications link in connecting the smart city. Upskilling postal employees and linking state-owned enterprises are key in providing a low-risk approach to implementing the smart city that reduces inequality. This increased role of the PO will empower its employees and the communities that the post offices serve. Linking the PO to an e-governance strategy is key to holding elected officials accountable in the smart-city rollout.

THE PUBLIC, OPEN-SOURCE-MOTIVATED SMART CITY

Maker spaces, open-source software and hardware efforts, and crowdsourcing provide a bottom-up alternative to the design and implementation of the smart city.[2] Universities, non-profit organisations (NPOs) and non-governmental organisations (NGOs) can contribute directly to this effort. This decentralised approach has the

---

2 T. Alizadeh, Crowdsourced Smart Cities versus Corporate Smart Cities, *IOP Conference Series: Earth and Environmental Science*, pp. 1–20 (IOP, 2018)

potential to unleash the most creativity and is focused more on job creation. The PO installations can become sites for community engagement, training and the location of start-up projects. Tshwane University of Technology (TUT) in South Africa has initiated a technology-transfer project that engages local post offices as sites for community technology exchange related to water, energy and industry. This is an opportunity to infuse the smart-city concepts in smart buildings, starting with the PO locations associated with the TUT project. Each PO location could serve as a hub supporting smart-city projects in the surrounding communities.

CONCLUSION

Both government and open-source scenarios rely on the post office playing a key role. The corporate scenario has dominated much of smart-city development. This approach has the backing of major multinational corporations and with significant financial resources can potentially dominate the smart-city future. However, the corporate scenario favours privatisation and could lead to dismantling of postal structures that are state-owned enterprises. The government scenario relies on government linking the state-owned enterprises and requires a stable tax base and citizen support. There is the risk of imbalance of delivery when the city is controlled and directed by an elite, more privileged sector. The open-source scenario of the smart city focuses on community control. It has the potential for benefiting the broadest base. It would require the injection of financial and human resources into the most disadvantaged sectors. This is where universities, civic organisations and non-profit projects can play a particular role in using the smart city to combat inequality.

QUESTIONS FOR THOUGHT AND DISCUSSION

1. *How can the PO and its regional and international organisations promote the development of a sustainable smart city?*

2. *The reality of smart-city development is a complicated mix of the different scenarios outlined. What are the factors that will determine which approach will have most influence, and what role can small and micro businesses and entrepreneurial start-ups play?*

"Existing models are ripe for innovation and many national posts have the know-how and capability to deliver ground-breaking innovation."

TRULY SUSTAINABLE DISRUPTION IN THE LAST MILE

Alberto Pereira

Bluecrest

INTRODUCTION

National posts are looking to define their relevance and value in a borderless, digital, e-commerce world. But how do they do this in an increasingly competitive and fluid market where margins are wafer thin? The answer lies potentially in embracing and welcoming change from innovation that truly delivers sustainable delivery solutions.

Existing models are ripe for innovation and many national posts have the know-how and capability to deliver ground-breaking innovation. An interconnected circular economy of sustainable business practices can not only secure the future of the post but be a true leader in tackling the central problem we all face: climate change. An issue we cannot self-isolate from.

CRACKPOT IDEAS?

In December 2019, the *Financial Times* ran an article on how tunnels can overhaul how our shopping is delivered. The article recounts an anecdote of how businessman Roger Miles, in 2003, was told by officials within Her Majesty's government that "they do not invest in crackpot ideas".

All too often, true innovation is considered to be a bit 'crackpot'. Weren't the Wright brothers crazy for suggesting flight? How many wrote off Apple in 2007 – a PC company, no less – for entering the phone market with a touch screen?

As we enter a new era post-COVID-19, do we need to ask ourselves whether the last mile really needs more than just a cargo bicycle and an electric vehicle to solve the complexities around cost and carbon footprint? Where are the 'crackpot' ideas in this digital landscape that can transform the last mile and even contribute to solving mankind's central problem for tomorrow: climate change? COVID-19 has highlighted the need to prepare for events that, if dealt with now, can be far less costly when they occur; and despite the ravages of the pandemic, it has been an engine for innovation and discovery.

The World Economic Forum in January 2020 released a roadmap that documented some of the challenges that the last mile will encounter in the coming years. It states that to "satisfy customers' ever-rising desire to buy products online, the number of delivery vehicles in the top 100 cities globally will increase by 36% until 2030. Consequently, emissions from delivery traffic will increase by 32% and congestion will rise by over 21%, equalling an additional 11 minutes of commute time for each passenger every day."[1] To exacerbate things further, these issues do not occur in an orderly and linear framework. Instead, they are connected by a complex network of agents wooing customers with promises of faster delivery, and policy makers are cautious of implementing laws that might cause ripple effects in other areas of the economy.

There are two ideas that should now progress from the concept stage and move into the last mile for everyone to benefit from.

REVERSE LOGISTICS TO PROMOTE A CIRCULAR ECONOMY

The idea that we can continue to make, use and dispose of unwanted goods is dated and unsustainable in a world where the global population is estimated to reach over 9 billion in 2050.

A circular economy proposes the notion that resources are kept in use for as long as possible to extract the maximum value from them whilst in use, then at the end of their service life, they are recovered and used to regenerate products and materials.

In a paper written by professors Terence Tse, Khal Soufani and Mark Esposito of the Centre for Circular Economy at the University of Cambridge, the authors argue that national posts have the reach and infrastructure to promote circular initiatives within reverse logistics.[2] How? By utilising national posts' daily touchpoints within

---

1   Deloison et al., 2020

2   Esposito et al., 2017

the last mile and acting as collection agents for unwanted goods. These can then be taken directly to local facilities for sorting to onward recovery plants, remanufacturing centres and/or manufacturers that will turn the unwanted items into new goods for onward sale.

Maybe the dialogue within our industry should shift away from the declining profitability in delivering parcels within the last mile, to the idea that our national posts can find new purpose and value by offering a service that can quite literally make a world of difference. CMO and CFO for the IPC, Mr Tom Day, was quoted as saying in his former role within the USPS as head of sustainability: "We reach out to nearly 153 million addresses 6 days per week. It takes minimal effort to take back a product that is no longer needed by the customer, especially if this product is below 10 lbs."[3]

Society plays a vital role in the success or failure of circular economics. Consumers, studies show, would prefer to cast aside an item to be collected by the refuse truck for landfill, rather than drive the item to a drop-off centre for recycling.

Commercial sustainability and longevity of our national posts within the last mile are at threat. Reverse logistics to promote a circular flow of goods for re-use, remanufacturing and refurbishing not only offers new revenue streams, but also offers the opportunity to make a real difference for tomorrow's world.

SUPERSONIC TUNNEL DELIVERY

Right up until 2003, Mail Rail in the UK transported items of mail to sortation centres in the Greater London area via a dedicated underground railway. Delivering around four million mail pieces per day throughout the Second World War and right up until the early 2000s, it was argued that Mail Rail removed mail trucks from congested roads, up to 80 trucks per week according to a report by the Greater London Authority. The argument was lost, and Mail Rail now acts as a tourist attraction.

Around the same time as Mail Rail's demise, Elon Musk was proposing Hyperloop to the world, moving people at high speed in a tunnel between California and Las Vegas. As with most good ideas, timing is everything, and today Magway, a UK-based firm, proposes to take a 'crackpot' concept and make it a reality: a revolutionary goods and parcels transport system propelled by magnetic motors, utilising existing pipe technology to connect distribution and consolidation centres.

---

3   Esposito et al., 2017

Cost, technology limitations and/or installation challenges are reasons some believe this will never come to fruition. I disagree with them, for three reasons:

1. THE DISRUPTION IS NOT SO DISRUPTIVE

Pipe technology and the installation of pipes across the globe are well known and not nearly as disruptive as many claim. Established and congested cities that make up the last mile quite often have an entire hive of activity happening below the surface. From installing utilities like gas and water, to broadband internet cables, the idea that cities need to be dug up to lay a pipe is wrong. In addition to that, who says a pipe even needs to be underground? Proposals and concept videos show pipes can be installed above ground – along train tracks or motorways.

However, whilst pipe technology is a bit old hat, what is going on inside the pipe is truly ground-breaking technology. A linear motor that propels a tote along a pipe carrying up to 30kg of goods can shift about 12 million totes per week.

Sustainable last-mile technology today consists of EVs to reduce emissions, but it does not solve the issues of size in certain truck categories, the cost of electrifying and charging, supply-chain vulnerabilities or congestion in our urban areas.

The 'last mile' is typically about 50 miles from port or airport to inner-city warehouse, and then onward to home, parcel locker or PUDO. Should the last mile not be around five miles for onward completion of a delivery by bike, EV or even drone?

2. BLUE-SKY THINKING AS THE NORM, NOT THE EXCEPTION

In today's digital landscape, technology and innovation will solve some of the last mile's biggest challenges. Large established incumbents will recognise that tunnelling may very well be a threat to their existing business activities. Forward-thinking CEOs will recognise that ideas do eventually become reality, and will happen with or without them. No one wants to be the next Blockbuster, shunning the new Netflix.

3. CRITICAL MASS

World-changing ideas require critical mass. Where conversations, in the beginning, happen in isolation, eventually dots are connected, and suddenly there is a groundswell of momentum. The success of circular initiatives will rely not only on collaboration of different experts and sectors to solve complex issues, but on all of us: as consumers, investors and global citizens. There are signs that this momentum is now taking place. Companies like Magway are being funded not by large institutions or venture capital, but instead by more than 2,000 retail investors, who have bought into their vision for clean, sustainable and affordable delivery.

CONCLUSION

On the grounds of sustainability and the environment, we need to welcome concepts like reverse logistics and tunnel delivery into discussions on the future of the last mile. The reality is that they can also be the biggest commercial opportunities the sector has yet seen. Our ambitions should be bold.

The groundswell of momentum is happening. You'd be crackpot not to sit up and get involved.

QUESTIONS FOR THOUGHT AND DISCUSSION

1. *How can 'crackpot ideas' be more quickly adopted and momentum built to a critical mass? In the world of social media and viral campaigns, is this easier or harder?*

2. *Is the postal world taking climate change seriously enough? What can it do?*

REFERENCES

Deloison, T., et al. (2020) 'The Future of the Last-Mile Ecosystem', World Economic Forum.
Esposito, M., et al. (2017) 'Reverse logistics for postal services within a circular economy', Wiley.

"Sustainability is no longer an option or a 'nice to have': it is an essential part of everyday operations."

A SUSTAINABLE FUTURE FOR LAST-MILE DELIVERIES

Angela Hultberg

Ingka Group (IKEA Retail)

INTRODUCTION

What we have been through in 2020, and continue to go through in 2021, has affected us all, both as people and as businesses. The pandemic has changed so much in our everyday life, and for businesses, years of progress had to happen in a few months for us to survive. Many who did not have the means to adapt so swiftly went out of business. Now, when the end of the tunnel seems to be getting closer, we must all reflect on what has really happened, and make sure we learn the lessons we have just been taught.

The pandemic made online sales explode. At IKEA Retail we saw massive increases in all markets, regardless of the level of restrictions, lockdown or no lockdown. Online sales really did save us during a time when most of our stores were closed, but not without a huge effort to turn stores into fulfilment units, find the transport capacity we needed and ensure workers were safe while doing so. But even as countries started to open up again, albeit with some restrictions, online sales have remained more than 50% higher globally than pre-pandemic. And lest we forget, until that point, every year was a record year.

For context, during Tertial 1 in FY21 (September–December) IKEA Retail performed as many deliveries as we did in the whole of FY20, which was itself a record-breaking year. This is the new reality for many retailers as consumers' shopping behaviours and expectations push for more and more deliveries. It is a whole new game, and one we must now decide how we want to play.

THE IMPACT OF DELIVERIES ON PEOPLE

With online sales come deliveries. And with deliveries come many issues we know we need to address. CO_2 emissions are of course a pressing matter. If we, as a society, are to have any chance of slowing the climate crisis down and limiting the global temperature increase in this century to 2°C, let alone 1.5°C, changes need to be made. But there are other issues too, like air pollution, noise pollution and congestion.

Air pollution was a huge problem already before the pandemic swept over the world. According to the World Health Organisation (WHO), over seven million people die of air pollution every year, and we also know that one-third of all strokes, heart disease and lung cancer are caused by air pollution. COVID-19 has demonstrated how poor air quality can make a horrible situation even worse, with studies from Harvard showing a direct correlation between COVID-19 cases and air pollution.

A study from the World Economic Forum, 'The Future of the Last-Mile Ecosystem', concluded that, at the current rate, the number of delivery vehicles in the top 100 cities would increase by 36% until 2030. Consequently, emissions from delivery traffic would increase by 32% and congestion would rise by over 21%, equalling an additional 11 minutes of commute time for each passenger every day. But that report came out in early 2020, before the massive increases in deliveries we now know to be our new reality.

Air pollution and climate change are two sides of the same coin. The main driver is the burning of fossil fuel. Most of what we do to mitigate one will also mitigate the other. The reduction of noise pollution is just an extra bonus. During this pandemic, we have gotten a glimpse of what a future without air pollution could look like. We have seen skylines that we have not seen in many years. People with asthma have been able to breath better than ever before. There are many examples which show that we should aspire for a new and better normal. However, all these benefits will be short lived unless we start making significant changes.

We simply cannot afford to keep polluting our cities, especially as that is where most people live. We cannot afford to continue to live in an environment that compromises our health. And we definitely cannot afford to make the situation even worse. We need to commit to a more sustainable future.

This is true not only for businesses, but also for policy makers. Many cities are looking to enforce low- or zero-emission zones, tolls on fossil fuel, restrictions and other remedies to lower air pollution in city centres. For a company depending on online sales, the business case becomes clear, as reaching the doors of customers is a prerequisite for staying in business.

WHAT CAN WE DO?

Many companies already have commitments and goals connected to reducing CO_2 emissions from transport, and now it is crucial that we stay committed, not using the pandemic as an excuse to pause, or to slow down efforts. If anything, we need to accelerate.

IKEA Retail has a target of *"100% electric or zero emission deliveries and services by 2025"*. The target was announced in 2018, and we stay committed to it. However, it is an expanding target, with volumes growing every year. What was 100% in 2018 is not 100% now; but even so, we must keep our eye on the goal.

To date, we have deployed electric vehicles in more than 20 countries. We know they can make sense everywhere, from Japan to France to the Unites States. China is by far our biggest success so far, with 90% of all deliveries being made using electric vehicles. We know that this will allow us to save costs long term, with electric vehicles being cheaper to own and operate due to lower fuel and maintenance costs. Also, many cities are aiming to become 100% electric in the coming years, and with each city we learn more, making it easier to scale our efforts globally.

That said, electrification is only part of the puzzle we need to put together. We need to address congestion as well, making sure that we do not add vehicles to the roads. Customer expectations need to be met, with a convenient experience being front and centre. Not wanting to waste any resources, we also need to be as efficient as possible, with trucks utilised to the full extent. Different modes of transportation, such as cargo bikes and electric barges, have been piloted already. Parcel lockers that can be replenished by night to reduce congestion, social entrepreneurs to address the social agenda, returns and packaging material – the list of issues, and possible solutions, is long. We need to work with all of it if we want to build a truly sustainable omnichannel network.

NEW INDUSTRY RELATIONSHIPS

Thinking about electrification specifically, it comes with some challenges. The transformation will not happen by simply ripping out combustion engines and replacing them with electric ones – if it were that easy, I think we would be done by now. All companies that are at the forefront of sustainable transformation will name the same barriers: the lack of electric vehicles, their performance, the cost of buying them, the lack of charging infrastructure (and the potential energy restraints) and the lack of relevant financial mechanisms to enable transformation. There is sometimes a sense of waiting in the industry, waiting for someone else to do their part before I get started on mine. But we cannot afford to wait anymore.

The roles of different stakeholders in the industry are changing. IKEA Retail is a buyer of transport services. We rely on our transport partners to deliver our goods to our customers, and we do not own a fleet of delivery vehicles. Even so, we find ourselves working directly with OEMs, co-developing vehicles suitable for a company like ours. We are working with leasing platforms to enable our transport service partners to go electric. We are building the charging infrastructure we need ourselves. Our role as a buyer of services has changed since we set the ambition in 2018, and it will continue to do so as the industry is reshaping.

New partners and new relationships are being forged as we address the challenges head on. Old 'truths' need to be challenged: we can no longer rely solely on what history tells us and we now need to find new ways of working. When the world is changing, we must change with it; not doing so means going backwards.

CONCLUSION

The last mile must become more sustainable, or cities will soon be too unhealthy to live in. As local policy makers are trying to make life better for their constituents, doing better in the last mile is simply a prerequisite for business. Sustainability is no longer an option or a 'nice to have': it is an essential part of everyday operations.

The transformation of the industry is not something that is about to happen or is happening soon. It is happening now. New partnerships are being formed, new solutions deployed and scaled up. The industry is reshaping, and companies must decide what role they will play in this more sustainable future. If not, they might not have a future at all.

What will you as a business bring to the table? What do you have to offer? What lessons have we learned in this tumultuous time for last mile? Last-mile deliveries should be part of making life better for people, not making their surroundings unhealthy. A truly sustainable last-mile setup is within reach, but only if a critical mass is committed to getting there. The future we want can only become reality if we build that future together. What will be your contribution?

QUESTIONS FOR THOUGHT AND DISCUSSION

1. *We see here a clear commitment from a major retailer to a more sustainable last mile. How does this contribute to the wider imperative for all operators and carriers in the last mile? How can the efforts of all those operating vehicles in the last mile be integrated and scaled up in a complementary way, rather than simply contributing to yet more urban congestion?*

2. *What is your response, for your organisation, to the questions posed in the final paragraph of the conclusion?*

REGULATION TO UNDERPIN BUSINESS SUSTAINABILITY

"The regulation surrounding these options will... determine if the sector, by 2030, is characterised by healthy profits, actual or impending losses, dynamic competition or segments dominated by single operators, and whether it is meeting the needs and expectations of future users with regard to universality."

REGULATORY OPTIONS FOR UNIVERSAL SERVICE OBLIGATIONS (USO) FOR THE SECTOR IN 2030

Ian Streule

Analysys Mason Limited

INTRODUCTION

The year 2030 seems a long way from today – nearly a decade away. Ten-year forecasts are always subject to some degree of uncertainty. This uncertainty can lead to forecast error. However, in the case of the postal and parcel sector, the consistency of historical trends should lead us to a generally acceptable forecast of the future.

A central long-term forecast for the sector can therefore form the basis of sector policies and highlight universal service regulatory options which will have to be considered between now and 2030.

These options will fundamentally shape the postal, parcel and supporting logistics sector over the coming decade. The regulation surrounding these options will also determine if the sector, by 2030, is characterised by healthy profits, actual or impending losses, dynamic competition or segments dominated by single operators, and whether it is meeting the needs and expectations of future users with regard to universality. Primarily, those needs are the availability, accessibility, quality and price of essential postal, parcel and logistics services for all residents and businesses.

WHAT CAN WE ANTICIPATE BY 2030?

Postal volumes, parcel volumes and supporting logistics are the three trends which should form part of any central projections for the sector.

POSTAL VOLUMES

Traditional letter volumes have been in steady decline for many years – a worldwide trend. In many countries, **declines of approximately 4% per annum**[1] do not sound dramatic, but compound mathematics means they will give substantial weakening of demand over a decade or more.

There has been debate on whether much of the remaining letter volumes are 'statutory', and therefore inelastic and not subject to volume decline. However, maturing consumer preference and acceptance of electronic statements, and corporate and government digitalisation efficiency programmes, do steadily reduce demand for traditional regular mailings. Evidence from countries such as Denmark shows that a historical reliance on letters for government business and private transactions can be broken, leading to a fraction of the peak letter volumes once enjoyed by the sector: Danish letter mail has reduced by more than 88% from 1998 to 2017.[2]

PARCEL VOLUMES

Measured volume growth in the formal parcel-delivery segment varies country by country, depending on the nature of local and cross-border (e-)commerce and home delivery solutions. In some countries, the informal sector enjoys most of the growth: for example, motorcycle couriers working Uber-style to pick up and drop off consignments, controlled by artificial intelligence (AI) routeing, consolidation and scheduling.

However, for many years, parcel volumes have **sustained average growth rates of 5–10% per annum**.

E-commerce, and the parcel volume growth it has stimulated, has also turned the postal, courier, express and parcels segments into a more complex and dynamic environment. Global players, local technology companies and financial institutions

---

1   Source: typical developed markets, data from the Universal Postal Union (UPU) and regulatory authorities
2   Source: Falch and Henten, Universal Service in a Digital World: The Demise of Postal Services, *Nordic and Baltic Journal of Information and Communications Technologies*, September 2018, pp. 207–22

are all keen to explore, and invest in, myriad sectoral and adjacent opportunities: robotics, AI, parcel lockers, handheld technologies, drones, food delivery and, importantly, horizontal and vertical consolidation.

SUPPORTING LOGISTICS

Advancements in logistics and technology to support packet and parcel volumes are an increasing focal area for the sector and its suppliers, with multiple announcements on a weekly basis.[3] The key developments are threefold:

First, *faster connectivity, greater capacity and improved (cost) efficiency* for all domestic and international road, rail, sea, air and through-customs transits.

Second, **sorting and fulfilment facilities**, using large machines and even larger well-connected logistics hubs. Integration with adjacent services such as the grocery chain is emerging.

Third, **delivery point technology**, including parcel lockers, smart locks, pick-up/drop-off (PUDO) points, and all the associated tracking, customer service and courier/vehicle control applications.

In some cases, advanced technology is being designed also to handle letter volumes. However, the rationale for developing complicated new technology for the declining letter segment seems narrow. There is no evidence that the lack of technology is constraining letter volumes per se, as there is a fundamentally downwards demand driver, so the benefits of investment will be around human resources cost savings and consumer utility benefits.[4]

IMPLICATIONS FOR 2030: CONVERGENCE AND CROSS-OVER BEYOND

The simple and sustained volume trends for letters and parcels mean that the sector is heading towards a convergence where the number of parcels and letters carried is similar, and the priorities of the whole sector will have shifted firmly away from traditional letters. Figure 1 highlights the situation for the UK, where the number of letter items per person-week has fallen significantly and appears to be approaching convergence with parcels in around ten years from now. Other countries will likely be much closer to the point of convergence, as the UK has a historically larger

---

3   For example, at: https://www.parcelandpostaltechnologyinternational.com

4   For example, explained at: https://www.singpost.com/about-us/news-releases/singpost-commences-public-trial-smart-letterboxes

reliance on letter communications.

The chart compares items per person, as opposed to items per delivery point, alongside delivery days per week as a measure of *individual utility*. The economics of delivery are related to this, albeit affected by the number of residents per household – but this is a more complicated analysis of fixed and variable costs not explored here.

During the same historical period, universal service delivery standards have been remarkably stable, shown in Figure 1 for the UK. Many countries have decided to implement reductions in the list of services considered as 'universal'. However, fewer countries have reduced the delivery frequency requirements for universal services – for example, enabling the number of home delivery days per week to be reduced substantially below 5 or 6, down to 1–3 days per week, particularly for economy or non-priority mail.

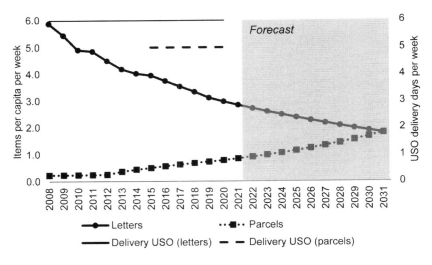

Figure 1. Trends in letter and parcel volumes and universal service obligation (USO) standards in the UK [Source: Ofcom, Analysys Mason]

With the consistency of historical trends in mind, the question is therefore not if but when convergence in volumes will happen. After convergence, there is likely to be a cross-over, because the trends in volumes are independent.

As illustrated, in a country with relatively high letter usage, this might be ten years away. In other markets, five years is indicated by the trends. Some countries might already have reached this point, particularly in the circumstances where COVID-19 has caused letter mail to decline, due to closed business activity, and parcel volumes to skyrocket as a result of e-commerce and home deliveries to working-from-home households.

ADDITIONAL CONSIDERATIONS TO TAKE INTO ACCOUNT

From a regulatory perspective, the anticipated trends mentioned above are only part of the relevant context. The approach to the postal, parcel and logistics sector should consider additional issues which are weighing in on the future development of technology and services.

Broader National Policies – These introduce both opportunities and threats. Environmental impact reduction must be addressed economy-wide – it is easy to point at inefficiencies due to numerous and/or part-empty delivery vehicles, which can be straightforward to tax accordingly. However, displacement activities must be factored in. CO_2 reductions in one business activity sound great but are probably useless if consumers or other businesses pick up the displaced activity and re-generate or generate net additional CO_2. Such topics are likely to be relatively new for communications regulatory authorities, although adjacent transport regulators will be well versed in their effects.

New Economic Bottlenecks are Emerging – As the parcel sector grows in importance and new delivery solutions are deployed, a variety of bottleneck concerns become relevant.

First, and today most obvious, is the increasing congestion of roads used for local delivery. Negative externalities arise for our air quality, driving times and pedestrian safety. Roads are an obvious physical bottleneck, but road-, congestion- and vehicle-based taxation are all effective regulatory solutions to manage demand, enabled by better information and technology.

Second, the public realm is itself a limited resource. Parcel lockers can be deployed in indoor and outdoor public space such as streets, social housing and railway stations, as well as in privately owned, publicly accessible locations such as shopping centres. In public spaces, a coordinated (i.e. regulated) solution may be required to avoid unsightly duplication of infrastructure or a land grab for prime sites by firms with profit incentives. The amenity (de)valuation of public space is particularly difficult to quantify.

Market Failures – A competitive market can provide many things, but there could be specific market failures in key areas. The parcel sector is considered reasonably competitive in most markets, and this competition gives rise to innovation and investment to differentiate.

However, the competitive supply market is likely to fail to (fully) provide equivalent services in uneconomic areas such as rural regions or economically disadvantaged suburbs. While this is often the case with national service provision activities, if a service is considered 'necessary' to support economic, social or educational inclusion (such as cash machines or broadband internet), then a universal obligation may need to be placed on a selected provider. This obligation generally exists already for postal and parcel services, but the key regulatory question is whether this is well fitted for the sector now, or in five to ten years.

As infrastructure requirements also increase, particularly around parcel locker deployments and super-sized warehousing, fixed and sunk costs will increase and the competitive economics will change. Competitors may consider closed networks and vertical integration to be the best way to limit competition in the long term. Combined with the presence of global giants such as Amazon and Alibaba, both horizontal and vertical aspects of services and infrastructure in the postal, parcel and logistics sector may need to be regulated in some way, in addition to the application of (ideally) longer-term merger-control competition economics.[5]

REGULATORY OPTIONS FOR THE USO

The sector trends and wider considerations discussed above will underpin the stability of, and changes needed to, the regulation of universal services in the postal and parcel sector. The options available to regulators include a variety of key 'levers'. However, given the transition of the sector from one dominated by letter volumes towards, and beyond, a parcel-centric industry, the nature of regulation and de-regulation will need a more nuanced, dynamic approach and careful planning over a long-term timeframe. However, joint planning for letters and parcels is needed, as there are significant shared costs and spill-over effects between letters and parcels in some parts of the sector.

Regulatory options include the following major aspects.

---

5 For example, this is being considered by the Swedish Competition Authority. See: https://www.konkurrensverket.se/nyheter/uppdrag-att-folja-upp-utvecklingen-inom-e-handeln-i-sverige

1. REDUCE FREQUENCY OF UNIVERSAL DELIVERY SERVICES

Reducing the frequency of universal service delivery to the door (home) primarily aims to give the designated postal operator greater freedom to adapt and reduce its cost base according to the mix of services and traffic.[6] In theory, universal delivery frequency could be adapted on a scale of 6, 5, 4, 3, 2, 1 days per week. However, there are complex and country-specific consumer and network management issues around fixed or alternating delivery days, the importance of weekend days, transit and storage, as well as the magnitude of any cost savings. This means that choosing stepwise or partial options might be less effective than simply aiming for a 'final' option further in the future.

2. REFLECT CHANGING NEEDS FOR SPEED, TRACKING AND TECHNOLOGY

Universal service requirements should aim to capture the necessary features of nationwide accessible, available and uniformly priced services for all residents and business users. In relation to *faster* speed, *accurate* tracking and *better* technology, these are becoming more 'necessary' for consumers, but the option to be determined is what level is necessary for universality, and what price – hence affordability – does this imply.

3. REFLECT CONSUMER PREFERENCES AND FLEXIBILITY FOR THE LOCATION OF DELIVERY

In many less-developed countries, the possibility to accept letter and parcel delivery away from home, at a PO box suite, has been the normal delivery solution. Conversely, developed countries have typically had nationwide universal delivery to the door, built on the foundation of traditional letter-mail services. There is a clear shift in consumer willingness to accept or prefer new delivery locations, and associated consumer flexibility to choose different options for different items. The willingness to pay for delivery nearer to the home, or to make savings for further-from-home delivery, is also evolving, particularly as consumers consider the benefits of certain delivery to a parcel locker or PUDO, compared to uncertain delivery to an unoccupied home. The interesting aspect of this is that some countries (such as Qatar) are introducing paid-for home-delivery services, while other countries are preparing for the option or default of lower-priced delivery to neighbourhood pick-up points. The chosen solution for universal letters compared to universal parcels is likely to be different.

---

6   A good example of this is the introduction of alternate-day delivery non-priority letters in Belgium, delivered only on alternative days to each address.

The specification of this delivery location nationwide is a detail which needs to be set: how near is the necessary location to the recipient's home (address)? The answer to this varies considerably in urban and rural areas, and depends on the potential exclusions of the last 5%, 1% or 0.1% of population. Delivery to a point within 300m can be considered acceptable in densely populated city areas; however, rural specifications are more likely to be around how long it takes to drive to the local pick-up point.

4. MODIFY OR CONTROL THE COMPETITIVE INDUSTRY STRUCTURE

The universal service obligation is itself a modification of the industry structure which would otherwise arise. Furthermore, the way in which a USO might be sustained, if it has a material cost, has to be set out. If the support for the USO involves in-market activities, these should be analysed or designed with an understanding of any related distortions. These can include the effects of reserved areas, and whether exclusionary practices or (unfair) cross-subsidies arise from other services (inside or outside the sector).

However, regulatory options around the industry structure needed to deliver and improve a future universal service can go further than conventional USO models.

Due to economic bottlenecks, negative externalities and competition distortions, greater control of the industry through licensing could be embraced. Requiring service providers to utilise specific infrastructure, or taxing the use of certain other infrastructure or services, can tilt the sector towards meeting broader specific universal objectives.

This is where universal logistics providers could be relevant – the adoption of universal, uniformly priced transport and delivery infrastructure services. City logistics models are another way that congested urban areas may, in the future, realise greater efficiencies and improved urban environments. This can be done through licensing and/or the obligation to consolidate volumes during conveyance, potentially using autonomous and electrically powered vehicles, through to a national infrastructure of delivery points, such as a pervasive deployment of standardised parcel-locker points.

CONCLUSION

The regulatory options that need to be selected for the postal, parcel and logistics USO in 2030 should be prepared with long-term foundations. My recommendation to stakeholders here is to develop a decade-long action plan to combine these options for your specific circumstances, your sector priorities and the local consumer needs which can be anticipated over the next ten years. This regulatory action plan should meet postal, parcel and wider policy objectives and have the flexibility to adapt if the sector is moving more quickly, or more slowly, towards a future outcome.

QUESTIONS FOR THOUGHT AND DISCUSSION

1. *Will incremental changes be sufficient to sustain the postal USO or will the dramatic changes in the postal landscape (e.g. huge growth in parcel volumes, intense competition in the last mile, so-called urban 'cherry picking' from new entrants and the need for environmental sustainability) drive a more radical regulatory review of all delivery services relating to competition and universal service obligations?*

2. *Historically, regulatory activity has been a matter for national authorities and dealt with by sector. With many cross-border players now operating in the market and sector boundaries disappearing in the digital world, how might regulators and policy makers collaborate to address these developments?*

"If the parcels market is to truly deliver for consumers, we need a radical rethink of last-mile delivery and the regulation that surrounds it."

REFORMING THE REGULATORY FRAMEWORK FOR PARCELS AND LAST-MILE DELIVERY

Cara Holmes

Citizens Advice

INTRODUCTION

The UK B2C parcels market has grown by over 300% in the last ten years,[1] with consumers spending over £2 billion per week in October 2020, an increase of more than 400% compared to the same time ten years ago.[2] Consumers now truly rely on e-retail, not only for the occasional purchase, but for essential and everyday items. Parcel delivery really is our newest essential service.

But regulation and consumer protections have not adapted to rising volumes or changing consumer behaviour. They are becoming increasingly outdated and no longer reflective of the way consumers interact with the delivery market. In the UK, communications regulator Ofcom regulates the behaviour of the formerly publicly owned monopoly provider, Royal Mail, but leaves the activities of all other operators largely unregulated, and the major consumer protection legislation was written when we were spending less than half the amount online than we do currently.[3]

---

1   Estimation based on figures from Pitney Bowes (www.pitneybowes.com/us/shipping-index.html) and Apex Insight (apex-insight.com/product/uk-parcels-market-2020).
2   ONS, Retail Sales Index internet sales, www.ons.gov.uk/businessindustryandtrade/retailindustry/datasets/retailsalesindexinternetsales
3   Figure based on ONS Retail Sales Index internet sales, and introduction of the Consumer Contracts Regulations in 2013 and the Consumer Rights Act in 2015.

60%	**30**	**1**
of parcels are delivered by an unregulated operator	the number of days before a parcel is officially considered late	major parcel operator is a member of an Alternative Dispute Resolution service

Figure 1[4]

UNCHECKED GROWTH

Unchecked growth has caused harm not only to consumers but also to workers in the industry and the environment. Our research has consistently shown that consumers experience issues throughout the e-retail customer journey, from ordering to returns, with six in ten (59%) consumers experiencing at least one parcel delivery problem a year.[5]

The majority of issues occur at the delivery stage or when a consumer needs to make a contact or complaint if something goes wrong.

---

4   60% figure based on market share estimates from Apex Insight (https://apex-insight.com/product/uk-parcels-market-2020); 30 days is the default delivery period specified in the Consumer Rights Act 2015; and Royal Mail and CMS Network (London) Ltd are the only members of POSTRS the Postal Redress Service.

5   Citizens Advice, The market which isn't delivering, 5 December 2019, www.citizensadvice.org.uk/about-us/our-work/policy/policy-research-topics/post-policy-research-and-consultation-responses/post-policy-research/the-market-which-isnt-delivering

Figure 2[6]

These problems can cause consumers inconvenience, loss of time, anxiety and stress,[7] especially when it is not as easy as it should be to put problems with delivery right. Consumers regularly report that it is difficult to find contact information, responses are slow, they must make contact multiple times or are passed off to another company.[8]

I purchased a birthday gift for someone from a retailer. They claim that my package was delivered on 15 June but I haven't received anything. They also can't find any records in their system when I inquire about who signed for or received the parcel. Now the delivery company say they can't find the shipment reference I gave despite sending them the screenshot from their own website! The seller isn't taking any responsibility or initiative to trace my package, and they aren't willing to refund my money. I feel like I've been cheated.[9]

---

6   Graph originally published in Citizens Advice, The market which isn't delivering, 5 December 2019

7   Citizens Advice, The market which isn't delivering, 5 December 2019

8   Citizens Advice, The market which isn't delivering, 5 December 2019

9   Anonymised case study from Citizens Advice's Consumer Service Helpline

The pressure on delivery drivers is well documented.[10] As the last link in the delivery, supply-chain delivery drivers are under immense pressure to fulfil the promises made by retailers to customers. Pressure on delivery drivers can mean them working long hours, not taking breaks and ultimately providing a poorer service to consumers. And although parcel delivery companies are working hard to increase the numbers of staff, there is still a question mark over how well delivery drivers can cope with consumer demand.

Last week I delivered 15 parcels to the wrong street because I was falling behind and I got stressed out. That's when you start making mistakes.[11]

The transport industry is the biggest polluter in the UK, accounting for 28% of all greenhouse gas emissions.[12] With Black Friday alone estimated to have released around 429,000 tonnes of carbon emissions into the atmosphere,[13] there is no doubt that the delivery market causes environmental damage. There have been interesting innovations in this area with electric vehicles, cargo bikes and parcel lockers. But these interventions are almost all geographically limited and often only used by a single delivery company. Coordination and cooperation are needed if these new technologies are going to have any meaningful impact.

10   See: Robert Booth, DPD courier who was fined for a day off to see doctor dies from diabetes, 5 February 2018, www.theguardian.com/business/2018/feb/05/courier-who-was-fined-for-day-off-to-see-doctor-dies-from-diabetes; Moore and Newsome, Paying for free delivery: dependent self-employment as a measure of precarity in parcel delivery work, 2018, eprints. whiterose.ac.uk/130079/3/WES291217.pdf; Tom Wall, Driven to the edge: life on the Christmas parcel delivery run, 8 December 2019, https://www.theguardian.com/business/2019/dec/08/christmas-parcel-delivery-drivers-driven-to-the-edge

11   Quote from delivery driver from forthcoming research undertaken in October 2020

12   Department for Transport, Decarbonising Transport: Setting the Challenge, 4 March 2020, https://assets.publishing.service.gov.uk/government/uploads/system/uploads/attachment_data/file/932122/decarbonising-transport-setting-the-challenge.pdf

13   Salman Haqqi, The Dirty Delivery Report; counting the carbon cost of online shopping, 3 November 2020, https://www.money.co.uk/guides/dirty-delivery-report-2020

COVID-19

COVID-19 has led to a rapid and sustained increase in parcel volumes which has exposed the cracks in the market at the time when consumers are relying on it the most.

Before the pandemic, growth in the parcels market was steadily increasing year on year. But in March 2020, with shops closed and social distancing measures in place, consumers took to the internet like never before, with online sales predicted to overtake buying in store for the first time in December 2020.[14]

However, in an industry built on fine margins, this increase in volumes at a time when numbers of staff in depots have had to be reduced has led to an increase in consumer problems. Our Consumer Service helpline took almost 200% more calls about parcel delivery problems in May 2020 compared to the year before.

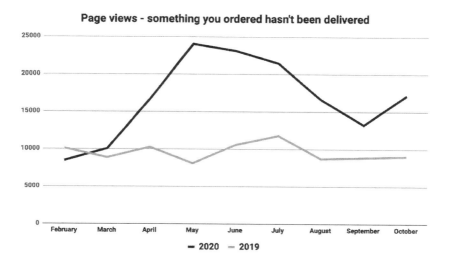

Figure 3[15]

14   ParcelHero, Lockdown 2.0 means home shopping will grow by 54.9% this month, 5 November 2020,   https://postandparcel.info/128618/news/e-commerce/parcelhero-lockdown-2-0-means-home-shopping-will-grow-by-54-97-this-month

15   Views to Citizens Advice webpage, If something you ordered hasn't arrived, https://www.citizensadvice.org.uk/consumer/somethings-gone-wrong-with-a-purchase/if-something-you-ordered-hasnt-been-delivered

In 2019, 3 in 5 (59%) consumers experienced at least one parcel delivery problem in 12 months. But since then, during COVID-19, issues have skyrocketed, with over 17 million (1 in 3) UK adults experiencing at least one parcel delivery problem in a single week in May.[16] And despite COVID-19 measures being in place for some time now, these numbers remain high months into the pandemic.

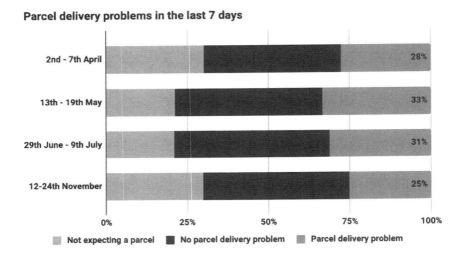

Parcel delivery problems in the last 7 days

Figure 4[17]

But these problems are not evenly distributed. Our research shows that it is time-poor and vulnerable people who are disproportionately affected by delivery problems. This includes people who are self-isolating, those with young children and those working irregular or unpredictable hours like carers and healthcare workers.

16   Figure based on ONS estimate of 52,673,433 UK adults and Citizens Advice research showing that 33.5% of UK adults had a parcel problem in the last seven days (research conducted 13–19 May 2020).

17   UK adults experiencing a parcel delivery problem in the last seven days. Base sizes vary across waves but are all a minimum of 2,000 respondents.

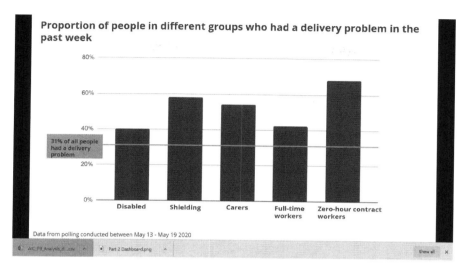

Figure 5[8]

Part of the reason for this discrepancy could well be time. Time to wait at home, to come to the door or to contact companies if something goes wrong. Our research shows that being out of the house was the reason almost 2 in 5 (39%) consumers missed parcels.[19] Of those, 40% were out for unavoidable work- or caring-related reasons,[20] going to show that when many of us receive over 100 parcels a year[21] we just don't have the time to be constantly available waiting for deliveries.

A RADICAL RETHINK OF LAST-MILE DELIVERY

If the parcels market is to truly deliver for consumers, we need a radical rethink of last-mile delivery and the regulation that surrounds it.

The parcels market in its current form is not working. Not for consumers, who are expected to be ready to open the door at a moment's notice; not for the workers

---

18   Kirstin Latimer, Christmas is on its way, but can the parcels market truly deliver?, 10 December 2020, https://wearecitizensadvice.org.uk/christmas-is-on-its-way-but-can-the-parcels-market-truly-deliver-81e3e729eacf

19   Previously unpublished Citizens Advice research carried out in September 2020

20   Previously unpublished Citizens Advice research carried out in September 2020

21   Ofcom, Residential Postal Tracker Tables Q1–Q4 2019, 17 February 2020, https://www.ofcom.org.uk/__data/assets/pdf_file/0022/191524/Ofcom-Residential-Postal-Tracker-Tables-Q1-Q4-2019-a.pdf

who have increasingly unmanageable loads to deliver; and not for the environment, as emissions associated with the last mile are ever increasing.

It will take radical change to address these issues and a level of coordination between government, operators and retailers that has so far been absent. This is the kind of coordination that regulation can provide. A set of regulatory principles would provide a clear consumer focus whilst still addressing the externalities of worker and environmental harm.

THE REGULATORY PRINCIPLES THE DELIVERY MARKET NEEDS

1. *INFORMED CHOICE*

Consumers too often are not provided with the information sufficient to make an informed purchasing decision. This can be a lack of information on consumer rights, whether there are options for specifying delivery needs, or details on the complaints process. When ordering items for delivery, consumers need informed choices, which means consistent, clear and comprehensive information provision throughout the purchase and delivery process.

2. *CONVENIENT DELIVERY AND RETURNS OPTIONS THAT CONSUMERS CAN HAVE CONFIDENCE IN*

Home delivery should be a convenient and safe alternative to in-store retail, but our research shows it can be anything but. Almost 1 in 5 (18%) consumers receive 'sorry we missed you' slips despite being in,[22] over 1 in 10 (13%) have parcels left in insecure locations[23] and 17% of disabled people have missed a delivery because they didn't have enough time to get to the door.[24]

Consumers need delivery and returns options they can rely on, no matter their personal circumstances. Convenience and confidence can be improved through the provision of local pick-up and drop-off (PUDO) points for delivery, collections and returns; fair pricing for those living in rural areas; and consistently providing the opportunity to specify additional

---

22 Citizens Advice, The market which isn't delivering, 5 December 2019
23 Citizens Advice, The market which isn't delivering, 5 December 2019
24 Previously unpublished Citizens Advice research carried out in August 2019

delivery needs. Increasing the use of PUDO points allows deliveries to be consolidated, which has positive impacts on both delivery drivers and the environment by reducing the number of failed deliveries and miles travelled.

3. *CLEAR CHANNELS OF COMMUNICATION*

Although consumer law is clear that it is the retailer's responsibility to resolve delivery issues, this is not always clear to consumers, who can struggle to get a resolution for delivery problems. This is made more difficult by the fact that some delivery companies are now contracted to handle contacts and complaints, making it even harder for consumers to know who is best placed to deal with their issues. Communication could be improved by proactively alerting consumers to delivery problems such as delay, damage or loss; increased communication through the returns process on status and timelines; and consumers receiving a consistent standard of service regardless of retailer or operator.

CONCLUSION

This regulatory reform is desperately needed not only to allow the market to meet consumer needs, but to do so without exploiting workers or the environment. The way we shop has changed forever, with 83% saying that they intend to continue or increase their levels of online shopping after COVID-19.[25] But despite this growth and increased reliance, there has been little to no change in regulation or consumer protections. Indeed, even though many consumers now receive multiple deliveries a day, the way we receive parcels still looks very similar to how it did when businesses with receptionists or loading bays were the main recipients of parcels.

If you were designing a market from scratch, this is not how it would look – a patchwork of different solutions often tied to individual delivery companies, with consumers anxiously waiting at home or wondering whether the items can squeeze through their letterbox while they are out. But smart regulation can help. Logistics is a delicate balancing act, and with the right regulatory framework, the market can deliver for consumers whilst also meeting the moral imperatives of respecting its workers and the environment.

---

25 Royal Mail, Almost half of UK adults have been receiving more parcels during the coronavirus pandemic, 22 May 2020, https://www.royalmailgroup.com/en/press-centre/press-releases/royal-mail/online-shopping-research-parcel-ordering

QUESTIONS FOR THOUGHT AND DISCUSSION

1. *Where should the impetus and ideas for reforming regulation come from – the regulators or the operators? Is there scope for self-regulation in the sector?*

2. *What is the best way to monitor and champion the voice of the end consumer, especially the disabled or those disadvantaged in other ways?*

"The question is not if regulation has a role to play in the last mile but when and to what extent."

LAST-MILE REGULATION – FRIEND OR FOE?

Graeme Lee

Sunflower Associates

INTRODUCTION

Does regulation have a role to play in the last mile? As e-commerce grows and grows, the visibility of last-mile solutions has been increasing at an equal pace. This has been exacerbated during the COVID-19 crisis and home delivery of packages, supermarket shopping and fast food is commonplace. My own small neighbourhood of 40 properties is serviced by one road and daily there will be a procession of vans from a variety of parcel carriers throughout the day. Added to that will be two or three supermarket delivery vans and in the evening a succession of fast-food deliveries.

Increasingly, particularly in cities, this motorcade of last-mile service providers is being seen as a spiralling nuisance that must be tackled. The question is not if regulation has a role to play in the last mile but when and to what extent.

WHO ARE THE LAST-MILE STAKEHOLDERS?

There are three main stakeholders in the last mile, each with differing and often contrary demands and priorities.

Customer   Operators   Society

The sending customer wants a carrier that will meet the needs of the recipient, taking into consideration price. The receiving customer wants a whole host of things including speed, convenience, tracking, timed delivery... all at a low price!

Operators want certainty over delivery so they can avoid having to redeliver items or having uncertain delays for making deliveries. It might be argued by some that operators would prefer to deliver to PUDOs or parcel lockers, but I am not sure that this is the case. It makes for a much easier operation but also makes for a cheaper solution, which will result in lower revenues.

Society wants to reduce congestion and the environmental impact of last-mile delivery solutions. However, the 'wants' of individuals often conflict with the 'wants' of society as a whole. An individual might want next-day timed delivery and choice but may also complain at the number of delivery vans on the road.

ARE PARCEL DELIVERIES SUFFOCATING BIG CITIES?

In a recent *Parcel and Postal Technology International* article, Rob Whitehead wrote on the topic of "addressing the issue of unsustainable parcel delivery in London". He asserted that "London is suffocating from too much road traffic" and a major cause was "the explosion in parcel deliveries" caused by increased demand for e-commerce. It was a thought-provoking article and certainly made me ponder his conclusions, some of which I fully agreed with and others which I had reservations about.

The assertion that parcel delivery is a major reason that London (or indeed anywhere) is suffocating seems a little unfair. However, if that assertion is true and, one way or another, we radically reduce the number of *parcel* deliveries, what about other last-mile deliveries? For example, what about supermarket deliveries or fast-food deliveries? The average parcel carrier will make about 80 drops per day on a full day excursion. In comparison, supermarkets will make about 15 drops on each of their two trips per day. Fast-food deliveries will be making single-digit deliveries and will make multiple trips per day. Reducing the carbon footprint or the congestion footprint of last-mile carriers is therefore more complex than it looks.

ARE PUDOS OR PARCEL LOCKERS THE ANSWER?

They are part of the answer but not the whole answer. At Post Expo, Doddle's Mike Richmond predicted that about 40% of items would be collected from PUDOs or parcel lockers and the remaining 60% would be delivered to the home. Also at Post Expo, Eduard Bockai made a very powerful presentation suggesting that customer expectation of the home delivery of parcels would become as high as our expectancy for running water or electricity. Personally, I concur with Eduard and wonder why anyone would want to collect an item if home-delivery solutions could provide a seamless, convenient solution that required no interaction from the recipient.

ARE MICRO-HUBS THE ANSWER?

Micro-hubs are an interesting concept and I think they are a good alternative solution to PUDOs and parcel lockers. The concept of the micro-hub is best exemplified by the ViaTim solution being introduced in the Netherlands. ViaTim is a network of very local delivery points that effectively act as an intermediary between the delivery company and the recipient. The delivery company delivers to the ViaTim agent and the recipient can either choose to collect their item or can pay an additional fee to have the item delivered to the home. In the case of ViaTim, delivery companies choose to work with them or not. If micro-hubs are to be the answer, delivery companies would need to be mandated to work with them and the micro-hub would then have a virtual monopoly on the last mile in its given area. Do we really want to have one monopoly provider of last-mile delivery in each area?

WHAT ABOUT SUPERMARKET DELIVERIES?

The demands on last-mile delivery for supermarkets are far greater than for parcel companies. In the case of online grocery shopping, the recipient has far greater control over the delivery window and date of delivery, and will pay for the service accordingly. A typical supermarket delivery vehicle will have capacity for approximately 15 drops, compared to the approximately 80 drops of a parcel carrier. The supermarket vehicle is likely to make two runs per day but that will still only equate to a maximum 30 drops. We can therefore surmise that the 'supermarket last mile' will have a greater environmental impact than the 'parcel last mile'. In which case, any last-mile regulation should consider supermarket deliveries.

WHAT ABOUT FAST-FOOD DELIVERIES?

Instinctively, I want to say that fast-food deliveries should not be considered in the scope of last-mile delivery, but I am not sure why. Companies such as Deliveroo and Just Eat are offering supermarket delivery in the UK, so why regulate one and not the other? The fact is that new delivery methods are making lines between different services blurred at best. Some posts are offering food delivery – even internationally, in the case of Japan Post; companies such as Amazon offer a wide range of ambient grocery products that are delivered as parcels; and now fast-food delivery companies are delivering small supermarket orders. On reflection, fast-food deliveries should be considered in any last-mile regulations.

WHAT ABOUT RUNNERS?

In a recent project in Brunei, we discussed whether there is a need to regulate runners or not. A runner is typically an individual that is employed to carry a package from point A to point B. In Brunei, runners are also employed to collect e-commerce items from just over the border in Malaysia, with buyers taking advantage of Malaysia's larger market and free in-country delivery. Brunei customers have their items sent to the nearest Malaysian post office, from which the runner makes the collection. Our view was that runners are, in many cases, providing what might be considered typical postal services and should therefore be regulated.

WHAT ABOUT ROUTE PLANNING?

At Post Expo, several companies were extolling the benefits of their route-planning algorithms, which could improve the efficiency of routes and even allow for in-route changes to take into account customer changes. However, such algorithms do not make efficient routes – they simply make very inefficient routes more efficient. One of the problems with supermarket deliveries is that customer time preferences must be shoe-horned into a route in a sub-efficient way. At least most parcel deliveries are done on the basis that routes are performed as efficiently as possible and recipients are informed of their delivery time after the route has been planned.

However, the problem is that every delivery company is effectively duplicating the same route in one form or another, resulting in optimal route planning for each operator but a very inefficient route plan overall. The most efficient route plan is one that would have one operator working on a fixed route every day – like the traditional route plans of incumbent postal operators!

ARE DELIVERY TAXES THE ANSWER?

Taxing deliveries is an answer – but what is the question? Would we tax deliveries in the hope that we will reduce the number of vehicles on the roads? If the answer is yes, then society should consider whether there are other taxes that would reduce the number of vehicles or have a greater societal impact. What about taxing parents that pick up their children from school every day? Not only would that reduce the number of vehicles on the roads, but it might also help to tackle child (and parent) obesity.

Would we tax deliveries in the hope of reducing environmental emissions? A better solution might be to specify that all last-mile delivery vehicles should be electric, thus reducing all emissions from delivery fleets.

Would we tax deliveries to promote collection of parcels? If all parcels went to a collection point within 250m of a person's home, what would be the proportion of recipients that would use their vehicle to collect the item? My guess would be that at least 50% of items under 2kg and 99% of items over 5kg would be collected using a vehicle.

CONCLUSION

Will last-mile regulation be a friend or a foe? Having no regulation results in the market setting its own rules and is likely to lead to operator-led and sub-optimal solutions. It may be good for the individual but not for society. Bad regulation can stifle the market and lead to poor quality of service and lack of innovation, of which there are many postal examples around the world. Good regulation can guide the market and take into account the many competing demands. It can find the balance between the needs of senders and recipients, operators and, most importantly, the needs of society as a whole.

The difficult challenge is how to provide good regulation for the last mile!

QUESTIONS FOR THOUGHT AND DISCUSSION

1. *The author concludes that regulation is necessary for the last mile. What are some of the ways it could be regulated?*

2. *What might be some of the challenges in regulating across different sectors, such as postal, retail grocery and fast foods, as well as small local trips like school pick-ups?*

POSTSCRIPT

Now you have had the opportunity to read the contributions in this book, I hope it has given you much to think about and enabled you to begin to explore how the sector is navigating the evolving digital landscape.

It is a good time to reflect again on the questions I posed in the introduction. You may now have some answers.

- How should the post, parcel and logistics sector position itself and be present in the 'always on' digital world we now all live in?

- What are the essential strengths, unique value propositions and particular expertise that we can bring to our service offerings, and how do we differentiate ourselves in a crowded and competitive market, such as the last mile?

- What is the role of our physical networks and customer touchpoints in the first and last mile, and how can we leverage these and integrate them into a seamless digital customer experience?

- What are the prospects for parcel volumes and letter volumes as we emerge from the pandemic, and if the significant shift from letters to parcels continues, how does that change our operational focus and business model?

- How do we retain and build our relevance, trust, breadth and reach in the evolving landscape?

- How do we react to the huge global digital platforms that are rapidly swallowing up market share?

- What are the opportunities for more collaboration and partnership with other businesses and organisations to consolidate more, share resources and consume less?

- Where are we finding innovation, fresh thinking and new ideas, and can we provide the platform and/or support for start-ups and small enterprises?

- How are the roles of regulators, stakeholders, owners and governments changing and impacting on our options, opportunities and business decisions?

- How will we emerge from the pandemic? Will we have learned important lessons and been able to refocus on a more sustainable future trajectory? Will we be more resilient and able to survive future shocks with better business-continuity plans in place?

- Finally, what role can we play, as a sector, to show leadership in sustainability initiatives and use our considerable environmental and business footprint to make a difference globally as a collective effort?

CONTRIBUTORS

John Acton has 30 years' experience in leadership roles within global organisations. As the executive vice president of the DPD Group, John was instrumental in driving the strategy that took DPD to being the undisputed kings of B2C across Europe. At the end of 2012, he set up the award-winning critical thinking consultancy, DPI, a uniquely different consultancy that harnesses its outstanding frameworks and facilitation to help leadership teams out-think their competition.

José Ansón is founder and CEO of UPIDO, a Swiss start-up delivering hyper-collaborative artificial-intelligence solutions for the last mile. He is also known for having created the UPU Integrated Index for Postal Development (2IPD), which is the ranking of the world's best postal services released every year on World Post Day. Jose holds a PhD in Economics from the University of Lausanne and is a postal and parcel big-data expert.

Dr Thomas Bayer is an experienced chief digital officer who has been working in the automation industry for over 20 years. He started his career researching in the field of AI and machine learning, and received his PhD in 1993. From 1998, he held senior management roles for Siemens and led regional businesses as CEO in the UK and US. Since 2020, he has been leading the digital business for the booming parcel market.

Stefan Berndt, based in Germany, has worked for the postal industry since 2003, and has provided all kinds of bespoke sorting solutions to the global postal market. Currently, he works as global business development manager for robotic solutions at Photoneo, which is a developer and producer of state-of-the-art 3D machine vision systems for vision-guided robots.

Stijn Braes is an economic advisor at the Postal Unit of BIPT (Belgian Institute for Postal Services and Telecommunications) and mostly works on dossiers regarding tariff regulation, analytical accounting and market monitoring. He has a background in academic research in the field of labour economics. He holds a master's degree in applied economics from the KU Leuven University.

Bernhard Bukovc manages the Postal Innovation Platform (PIP), an innovation-focused platform for the postal and logistics industry. He previously served as director of intercompany pricing and regulation at the International Post Corporation in Brussels and for the Austrian Post as director of regulatory affairs. He founded and manages Vinaficio, a European cross-border logistics, payment, tax and duty administration platform. He is also a consultant and founder of a start-up initiative.

Pierre-Yves Charles is legal advisor for the Postal Market Department of the Belgian Institute for Postal Services and Telecommunications. He holds a master's degree in law (Catholic University of Louvain 2001), and sat on the High Level Group on Internet Governance of the European Commission (2012–14) and the Governmental Committee of the Internet Corporation for Assigned Names and Numbers (2012–14). He is responsible for postal policy matters, especially the analysis of regulation on e-commerce and electronic postal services.

Alvin Dammann Leer is a serial entrepreneur and impact investor. Sustainability has remained a career theme, from honing his skills at the global NGO, the WWF, to studying social entrepreneurship in Boston and then co-founding two impact start-ups. Dammann Leer has held positions across three continents, as an editor and independent consultant for companies such as Innovation Norway, Adecco and the WWF. His educational background includes communication, behaviour change and social entrepreneurship.

Jean Philippe Ducasse has been a specialist with the US Postal Service Office of Inspector General since 2015. JP has worked since 1991 for major postal-sector organisations on both sides of the Atlantic (Pitney Bowes, the Universal Postal Union, the European Commission and Groupe La Poste). He has held senior positions in market research, strategy, international affairs and program management. jpducasse@uspsoig.gov

Originally at Metapack as an early employee, **Tom Forbes** re-joined the business in January 2014 as part of the executive team. He is responsible for Metapack's relationships with posts and carriers. Tom's 25-year career has all been in supply chain and he holds a master of arts degree from Oxford University.

Santosh Gopal has 25 years of management consulting and innovation, backed by entrepreneurial experiences. He has a strong technical background with experiences in creating start-ups in varied areas including education, media, healthcare, food and beverages, and publishing. His latest company, Ship2MyID, was built with keeping millennial and Generation Z shippers in mind. He speaks at several postal conferences and has gained significant mindshare to his newer transformational ideas that address several postal challenges.

Richard Hagen has been with Prime Vision from the beginning, early 2003. He has had various (managerial) roles within the organisation, such as general manager of the consultancy wing Prime Compete. Currently, Richard is responsible for new business development. He holds degrees in business administration, logistics, materials and supply change management.

Jack Hamande has been an executive board member of BIPT since 2013, was chairman of the European Regulators Group for Postal Services, vice chair of BEREC and had several leading positions within the UPU. He previously had management positions at the Walt Disney Group, AT&T, Verizon Business and Cisco. He holds a master's degree in psychological sciences (ULB) and a degree in management.

Wayne Haubner is a pioneering technology executive and change agent with a long track record of successfully building world-class customer-centric engineering organisations. Before joining Escher, Wayne occupied C-suite and senior-executive-level positions in the software, cloud computing and analytics space. Today, his experience in bringing leading-edge technologies to the market helps Escher transform posts into leaders in customer engagement. Wayne holds a degree in computer science from Eastern Kentucky University.

Cara Holmes joined the Citizens Advice Post and Telecoms team in 2017. Since then, her work has focused on consumer issues with parcel delivery, leading projects on all aspects of the market from complaints processes to regulatory reform. Before joining Citizens Advice, Cara held various positions in local government as well as teaching statistics and research methods for Cardiff University.

Angela Hultberg is the global head of sustainable mobility at Ingka Group (formerly IKEA Group). She leads efforts related to the sustainable mobility agenda, reducing customer and co-worker travel emissions as well as achieving zero-emission home deliveries and services.

Jacob Johnsen is founder and CEO of Ipostes, a postal expertise centre providing strategic, commercial and technical guidance to postal organisations worldwide.

He has helped some 30 national posts on five continents and is acknowledged for expertise in postal logistics and operations, including fulfilment centres, traceability and electronic messaging. Jacob is a popular contributor to the postal press, has authored and contributed to several books, and is a renowned speaker at many postal events. johnsen@ipostes.com

Alex Johnston-Smith leads Metapack's market research function, using Metapack data and research to support and develop understanding and opportunities in the carrier market.

Graeme Lee is a postal policy specialist with over thirty years' experience working in the postal sector on policy, regulation and strategy. A postal visionary and a veteran of working in more than 75 countries on postal projects, he has a truly global view on the main issues faced by the postal sector in the coming years.

Erwin Lenhardt is account executive for the postal and logistics industry at T-Systems, the IT division of Deutsche Telekom, supplying digital solutions, connectivity, cloud services and IT security solutions to large enterprises. Including his prior SVP positions with Siemens Logistics, he draws from more than 20 years of experience in the postal sector, supporting the development of major postal operators worldwide with close relations to many postal decision makers.

With a profound interest in computer science and a master's degree in software engineering, **Anders Lildballe**, lead software product architect at BEUMER Group, has had a leading role in turning data into an asset. Lildballe's team has pioneered predictive analytics, 3D visualisation tools and centralised machine learning as enablers to use data-driven information to optimise operations and drive greater efficiency for the parcel and baggage handling industry.

João Manuel Melo is team leader for Innovation Management (CTT Portugal Post's DTI directorate), leading for over two decades several I&D projects across CTT. Presently, he is responsible for managing a vast innovation program addressing trend analysis, exploratory innovation, start-up programs, ideas management, I&D and innovation funding. He has a degree in electrotechnical engineering (IST Lisbon) and qualifications in management and innovation (PAEGI, PAGE UCP Lisbon and PDE AESE Lisbon).

Padma Mishra is an Indian Postal Service officer and currently a course director at the Asian Pacific Postal College, Bangkok, Thailand. She has vast experience in India Post, working in operations and policymaking in national and international postal sectors. Before joining APPC, she was working in India Post as director of international relations and global business. She was an elected member of the QSF board of trustees. She has a master's in engineering.

Ethan Morgan joined Doddle in 2019 to deliver thought leadership, insight and analysis on e-commerce and the carrier market, and has previously worked on content strategy and marketing for e-commerce technology businesses.

Alberto Pereira is passionate about delivering innovation sustainably in the last mile. A master's graduate with a focus on technological change within disruptive environments, he works across EMEA with national and private postal carriers that share his vision for modernising and improving services to the communities they operate in.

Mike Richmond has been with Doddle since its launch in 2014 and is responsible for the company's relationships with parcel carriers globally. Mike is a qualified corporate and commercial lawyer, and worked in strategy and corporate development roles prior to joining Doddle.

Dr Eva Savelsberg is senior vice president of INFORM's Logistics Division. She specialises in optimisation software that renders a wide range of operational processes more productive, agile and reliable. Eva is also lecturer at the University of Aachen (RWTH), where she received her PhD in mechanical engineering in 2002. Eva has published five books and over 40 papers on innovation in freight transportation.

Markus Sekula is responsible for sales and key account management of INFORM's Logistics Division post and parcel customers. He brings over 15 years of parcel industry knowledge from his time with Hermes Group. He holds a master of science in transport management and logistics from the University of Applied Sciences in Bremerhaven.

Ian Streule has over 23 years' experience managing and directing consulting projects. He leads Analysys Mason's work in the postal and courier sector, including the development of postal- and courier-sector regulatory strategies in the Middle East, Africa and South-East Asia. Additionally, he has provided regulatory support to the postal regulators of the UK, Ireland and Belgium on regulated costing, pricing, QoS and universal service issues.

Michel Stuijt has worked in the financial sector for over 35 years. His experience is in corporate banking, international payments and cards. He also worked at an international IT company where he served the financial sector. In recent years he worked at Equens, the European payment and cards processor, and was CEO of

Eurogiro. Currently, with his consultancy firm Mozaiq Consultants, he advises Fintechs. He is also director of finance and risk at Rewire EU B.V.

John Trimble currently is a professor in industrial engineering at Tshwane University of Technology (TUT). From 2015 through 2016, he served as a Fulbright professor at TUT, while collaborating with the South African Post Office on research in postal innovation. He holds a PhD in industrial and systems engineering from Georgia Institute of Technology. He also serves as the president of the International Network on Appropriate Technology.

Holger Winklbauer has been IPC CEO since 2016. He is a senior executive with experience in strategy development, change management and consulting in logistics and the postal industry. Before joining IPC, Holger Winklbauer held several high-level positions within the Deutsche Post DHL Group. He also worked for the Metro Group, the Research Institute for Industrial Management and Mannesmann Anlagenbau. He studied electrical engineering and applied economics in RWTH Aachen University.

Matthew Wittemeier is senior manager, international marketing and customer relations at INFORM's Logistics Division where he has become a thought-provoking contributor to many industry publications and conferences.

Suhair Wraikat is head of the international relations department at Jordan Post, responsible for international relations and organisations, and participates in international postal events. With over 17 years' experience working in the postal sector, throughout her career she has also had extensive experience in compliance and financial departments. She graduated from the University of Jordan with a bachelor's degree in economics.

Yu Yan is the course director of APPU. She has over 20 years of related working experience in the postal sector. Studying the amazing growth of the CEP market and observing the massive disruption that happened to the postal sector, she has always been curious about what creates business growth, and what should be done to make great strategic planning, organisation restructure and regulatory policies in the area of postal reform.